What the World Should Be

What the World Should Be

Woodrow Wilson and the Crafting of a Faith-Based Foreign Policy

—Malcolm D. Magee—

BAYLOR UNIVERSITY PRESS

Scripture quotations are from the New Revised Standard Version Bible, copy-
right 1989, Division of Christian Education of the National Council of the
Churches of Christ in the United States of America. Used by permission. All
rights reserved.

Cover design by Donna Habersaat, dhdesign
Cover illustration is supplied by the Library of Congress. Used by permission.

Library of Congress Cataloging-in-Publication Data

Magee, Malcolm D., 1957-
    What the world should be : Woodrow Wilson and the crafting of a faith-
based foreign policy / Malcolm D. Magee.
        p. cm.
    Includes bibliographical references and index.
    ISBN 978-1-60258-070-1 (hbk. : alk. paper)
    1. Wilson, Woodrow, 1856-1924--Political and social views. 2. Wilson,
Woodrow, 1856-1924--Religion. 3. United States--Foreign relations--1913-
1921. 4. Christianity and politics--United States--Presbyterian Church--Histo-
ry--20th century. I. Title.

    E767.1.M29 2008
    973.91'3092--dc22

                                    2008010622

Printed in the United States of America on acid-free paper with a minimum of
30% pcw content.

Dedicated to
my Father and Mother,
Harold and Wilma Magee,
Who taught us that faith should be tempered by humility.

Contents

Acknowledgments

First among those to whom I am indebted is John W. Coogan, whose scholarship, friendship, criticism, editorial comment, and encouragement have made this book possible. I am also grateful to Sayuri Shimizu who provided helpful criticism and direction during a very challenging time at the beginning of this project. David Bailey, Werner Dannhauser, Amy DeRogatis, Simei Qing, Sam Thomas, Max Stackhouse, David Stowe, and particularly Calvin Davis read and provided valuable suggestions and criticisms of earlier versions of the manuscript. John Mulder deserves thanks for direction to sources on American Presbyterianism and Wilson. Mark Noll encouraged me in this work and commented on the abstract. I am grateful to Carey Newman and the wonderfully helpful and responsive staff at Baylor University Press for their willingness to undertake this project, and to Randall Balmer for recommending Baylor and encouraging me to send them my manuscript. Hal Bush and Roy Matthews deserve my thanks for support at various stages of this project.

Personal assistance came from too many sources to mention, and yet I will try. Thanks to Bryn Jones, who prior to his death pressed me to begin the path that includes this project. Also thanks to Alan Scotland, James Muffett, Mitch Bean, Rich Keener, Blaine Schultz as well as the congregation of Liberty Christian Church, my friends, for allowing me the time and space to continue work on this project. Thanks to Dr. Kurt Norgaard.

There are not words enough to say thank you to my assistant Karyn Coward who, following my crippling accident, ran errands for me, located material at the library, pointed out formatting flaws and generally acted as my legs until I could walk again. Your friendship and help will not be forgotten.

Thank you to my family, my children, their spouses, and my grandchildren (who provided the requisite grandchild distractions) and the extended family, who put up with me and sometimes even left me alone to work. Thank you: Katie, Jim, John, Kari, Kristin, Jeremy, Micki, Shelley, Curt, Simon, Eunhyun, Henry, Oliver, Thom, Jenn, Tony, Sherri . . .

Final thanks, however, must go to my wonderful wife Judy. Anyone who has been the spouse of someone obsessing over a manuscript will know what she has suffered.

Introduction

English economist John Maynard Keynes wrote, following the Paris Peace Conference, that Woodrow Wilson thought like a Presbyterian minister, with all the strengths and weaknesses of that manner of thinking.[1] Keynes, the chief economic advisor to the British delegation, who was present at many of the meetings with the president, condensed months of observation, personal interaction, and disappointment into this statement. He asserted that the foundation of Wilson's thinking about the world and international affairs did not rest upon a secular ideology or definition of national interests. It lay instead in his personal religious faith, a faith so absolute and pervasive that it determined not only what he thought, but also, more importantly, how he thought. Keynes argued that one could understand neither Wilson nor his policies without understanding his Presbyterian roots: intellectual, rhetorical, organizational, moral, and theological.

Keynes' insight is missing, for the most part, from modern historical scholarship concerning U.S. foreign relations during the Wilson presidency. Historians, trained to look at the evidence rationally, are challenged when encountering extrarational forces, including religion, at work in the subjects they study. It is tempting to ignore or marginalize these forces when trying to make sense of the record or fit it into some coherent theory. What to do, for instance, with a president who made decisions in the depths of depression, grief, or the euphoria of love, or while suffering the effects of physical breakdown. Wilson poses all of these challenges for the historian trying to interpret the thought process behind his policies. His religion,

1

however, does not pose the same difficulty for study, as he left an extensive record, both public and private, of his patterns of faith. The president's almost continuous association with Presbyterian institutions from his childhood until the end of his life allows the historian insight into the patterns of faith that undergirded and entwined themselves with Wilson's rational thought. In addition, he has left a written record of both public and private thoughts on his faith, which can be interpreted in the light of his long association with these institutions.

While religious faith challenges the historian, it is an essential (though not exclusive) factor in the study of Woodrow Wilson's foreign policy. Faith, intertwined with the president's reasoning processes, buttressed his thought and engaged his imagination of what the world should be. The specific patterns of faith became so integral to Wilson that they could not be separated from his reasoning. Those who worked successfully with the president did so by working within this pattern of thought. Those who did not were in varying degrees less successful.

What gives this subject even greater weight is the unique moment in history in which Wilson occupied the presidency. Growing American political and economic power, coinciding with Europe's suicidal war, put Wilson in power at the beginning of what would come to be called "the American Century." Wilson's policies influenced the future of American and global foreign relations for the rest of that century. Even subsequent policy makers who defined themselves as "realist" in their application of United States foreign policy, in an attempt to distance themselves from Wilson's *idealism*, continued, in the essentials, the Wilsonian element of American mission. Ultimately, Wilson's religion gave impulse to the image of the United Sates as a "redeemer nation." It also added strength to a particularly American foreign policy, based on faith in America's mission in the world, that continues to hold implications for American foreign relations.

Some historians dismiss this interpretation entirely, acknowledging that religious feeling was present in the president but asserting that it comprised little more than cultural evangelicalism. Among these are historians Niels Aage Thorsen, John Milton Cooper, and John A. Thompson. Of these, Cooper places the most importance on Wilson's electable + comfortable

religious views but argues that they remained separate from his secular profession. Cooper argues that Calvinist doctrines had little impact on Wilson, that his religious background created in him a humility about his ability to know the purposes of God, that he was not concerned about being a moral uplifter, and that he never became deluded into becoming a messianic crusader in politics.[2] Cooper has retained this view throughout the course of his scholarly career, repeating it in his most recent work on Wilson at Versailles and during the treaty fight with the Senate.[3] Thorsen takes this further, dismissing outright any emphasis on the religious influence in Wilson's political thought as *premodern*; religion was merely a rhetorical tool in his political career. To consider Wilson's religion leads away from his political thought, not toward it.[4] Thompson states it most bluntly: "Wilson's career cannot persuasively be interpreted as an attempt to reform human affairs in accordance with some higher, or Christian, ideal."[5] The president's politics were nothing more than America's secular ideology applied to international relations. These historians argue that conformity to nineteenth-century cultural evangelicalism made Wilson comfortable, his identification with an established and respected denomination made him electable, but religion had little or no impact on his political thought, policies, or actions in international affairs.

Even historians who endorsed Keynes' general observation have failed to examine the foundation of Wilson's complex and highly personal religious beliefs in order to explain their specific impact on international relations. Historians Jan W. S. Nordholt, Arthur Link, and John M. Mulder have argued that Wilson's religion was an integral part of who he was. Nordholt recognized that faith was fundamental to Wilson as a person and as a politician. He also argued that most historians fail to understand this because they have little understanding or even knowledge of the curious subculture that Christianity has become in the twentieth century.[6] Link wrote that Wilson's Christian faith was the basis for his understanding of the sources of power and his motivation to public service, that he was inspired to serve God by serving his fellow man. Faith in God and submission to the Christian ethic underlay all Wilson's political thought.[7] Mulder took the president's theological thought further. Writing what has been described as a religious biography of Woodrow Wilson, Mulder showed how ideas like *covenant* were tied to his Presbyterian upbringing. Mulder argues that much of Wilson's political thought had been formed by the religious family and Presbyterian world in which he came of age.[8] The focus of Mulder's work, however, was the years before Wilson entered politics. None of these historians apply specifics of how this influenced the way in which Wilson thought about international politics. Existing professional literature portrays a president variously motivated by idealism, realism, "higher realism," corporatism, ideology, personal ambition, or some combination of these. There has been no serious modern examination of Wilson's foreign policy in Keynesian terms: as a Presbyterian in politics, a twentieth century John Knox, a Christian statesman whose overriding motivation was his determination to do God's work in a fallen world.

Scholars of international-relations history continue to explain in almost exclusively secular terms the foreign policies of a man who himself insisted that faith was the foundation for all his international actions. Marxist historians such as N. Gordon Levin have even argued that religion was merely a pretense on the part of the president to establish a world capitalist economic order. The central and founding motivation was economic hegemony, not ideology.[9] Robert S. MacNamara and James G. Blight credit Wilson's grand vision for a new world to his secular life and experience in the post-Civil War South. They juxtapose this grand vision birthed by secular America with the narrow, petty, Presbyterian morality of the president that doomed it to failure.[10] This is consistent with much of the scholarly explanation which fails to see that there is no contradiction between the two visions in Wilson. They continue to explain in rational terms the foreign policies of a man who, when an aide suggested that his reparations policy had logical inconsistencies, snapped, "I don't give a damn for logic."[11]

Other scholars fall into variations of the categories of thought described above. Lloyd Ambrosius recognizes the existence of a religious tradition but places the foundation for "Wilsonianism" on the president's scholarship in history and American politics. He notes that modern scholars do not understand Wilson's use of language and often accuse him of hypocrisy, but argues the key is to be found in the president's scholarly record. He fails to note that this record itself is

some hist.
did not take a
closer look

founded on the deeper groundwork of the president's faith.[12] Religion professor P. C. Kemeny notes Wilson's comfort with religion in a secular context and how that fueled his views of educational reform while at Princeton. He does not look closely at how the future president's faith acted upon his thinking processes, which Keynes observed, and like Mulder, does not examine the Wilson presidency at all.[13] Edwin Weinstein and Kendrick Clements both note the president's tendency to view the world from a religious perspective. They, however, see that view as emerging only when the president's health was in decline and he was unable to approach the world from a more rational frame of mind. In this view Wilson's religion was a safe emotional place to go when his stroke incapacitated his greater mental faculties.[14] Thomas Knock, Daniel Stid, Phyllis Levin, and Margaret MacMillan provide further variations on the approaches previously discussed.[15]

This book is an attempt to let Wilson be Wilson, the man who throughout his life used such terms as *covenant* and *freedom* not in terms of their modern secular definitions but in terms of a very specific Calvinist rhetorical tradition, one largely unfamiliar today, especially among scholars of American foreign relations. The underlying assumption of this work is that to understand Wilson it is necessary to resist the tendency to see him in terms of twenty-first-century concerns such as corporate globalism or American unilateralism. Historians should seek instead to return him to his own historical context, that of the late nineteenth and early twentieth centuries.

The thesis of this book is that the future president was immersed in a particular Princeton and Southern Presbyterian tradition that he absorbed, quite literally, at the knees of his father, Joseph Ruggles Wilson, his devout mother, Janet Woodrow Wilson, and the religiously active clergy, family, and friends he was surrounded by from his youth onward. This tradition and these influences shaped the way Woodrow Wilson perceived the world. Indeed, as Link has written, it was almost as if Wilson was born with these convictions. They shaped his concepts of effective leadership and the way in which he used language. They shaped the way in which he reasoned, and in particular they accustomed him to the theological principle of antinomy: that two principles could both be right even when others, looking at them in the light of logic rather than faith, found them mutually contradictory. His

Presbyterianism made him believe that *law* was a living embodiment of personal conscience and spirit, not a rigid matter of words, statutes, and precedents. True freedom was obedience to divine order, and he used "covenant" not as an elegant synonym for "treaty," but rather in its full Old and New Testament meaning of nations and peoples accepting divine order in return for divine blessings. These convictions ultimately made him believe he was providentially chosen to bring that divinely ordered freedom to the nations and peoples of the earth, by peaceful means if possible but through force if necessary.

Religion is not the whole story of Woodrow Wilson. It is one thread in the tapestry. But it is the part of the tapestry of this complex, contradictory man least understood by current historians and least integrated into current scholarship on his foreign-relations policy. The task of restoring the president and his policies to the religious context that helped to form them, as stated, is difficult but not impossible. There is a substantial literature in the field of American religious history on Princeton and Southern Presbyterianism in the late nineteenth and early twentieth centuries. This literature is rarely cited in studies of his foreign policy, but is only one example of the resources that can be deployed profitably by the international historian. Other resources are denominational archives, such as the Presbyterian Historical Society's, which contain manuscripts and printed material specific to Wilson's tradition. The eyewitness accounts of those who worked closely with the president, found in their papers, provide further evidence of the religious character of Wilson's thought.

Before any new sources can be integrated effectively with prevailing scholarship, however, historians must become more comfortable with the reality of a believing, practicing, evangelical Christian in the White House. It is not easy for scholars trained in the secular, rational study of foreign relations to deal with a president who read his wife a poem—and effusively thanked its author—that compared him to David, King of Israel, and asserted that "His speech was voice of human man, His thoughts the words of living God."[16] Historians may find the language, tone, and content of such material uncomfortable and, indeed, embarrassing. But they cannot ignore it simply because it does not fit their own visions of a realist or an idealist or a liberal-capitalist or a progressive-internationalist or any of the other secular labels applied to Wilson.

Historian Andrew Preston wrote in the November 2006 issue of *Diplomatic History* that the gap between religious and international history ought to be bridged. While there should be caution in over-emphasizing religion, the imbalance of underemphasizing it is equally detrimental to the pursuit of history.[17] There has been a small surge recently in the examination of religion in politics. This has been largely prompted by the rise of the religious right in American politics during the late twentieth century. As a result of this renewed interest some authors have begun to speculate on the future of a religious left.[18] But those writing for the present tend to look for a usable past. Those looking into the past to find a future for religion, for whatever reason, will find much to use. The left in Christian politics also has a history. A history in which some would claim Wilson, William Jennings Bryan, not to mention Lyman Beecher, Walter Rauschenbusch, and many others. Religion in American politics has a robust history and promises to have a robust future. This book, however, is history, not prediction, and so does not speculate on the future.

1

The Development of Woodrow Wilson's Thought to 1913

On the morning of March 4, 1913 one thousand Princeton under-graduates escorted Woodrow Wilson from the Shoreham Hotel to the United States Capitol building to be sworn in as the twenty-eighth president of the United States.[1] The man taking the oath of office that morning, one of the most complicated individuals to occupy the White House, held a set of principles rooted in his faith that would eventually lead him to attempt the reorganization of the rules accord-ing to which the nations of the world interacted. He would seek nothing less than a complete overhaul of the system of international relations that had defined Europe, the West and their colonial posses-sions for centuries.

To understand Wilson and his approach to foreign policy requires an awareness of the religious convictions that informed his world view, his ideals, his assumptions and prejudices. His religion was inseparable from the other aspects of his philosophy. His biographer, Arthur S. Link, stated that faith was a way of life for Wilson. It never ceased to be so. He remained unshaken in this essential faith, despite the theological storms that raged around him during the later half of the nineteenth century. "Historical criticism and the evolutionary hypothesis, which he readily accepted, only strengthened his belief in revelation and the truth of scriptures."[2] God ordered the affairs of men after his own fashion. Faith in God was the means of mak-ing sense out of chaos. Faith gave ultimate meaning to the affairs of men. In December 1918, Wilson spoke to a group of Free Church leaders in London. "I think one would go crazy if he did not believe in Providence. It would be a maze without a clue. Unless there were some supreme guidance we would despair of the results of human counsel."[3] This religious world view was always present in Wilson; in times of crisis and physical breakdown the president found it a comfort, in his triumphs he saw it as the reason. Though it was always but one strand of his thought, its continuous presence influenced in some way all the rest.

This religious outlook on life came to Wilson as naturally as breath. Born December 28, 1856, in Staunton, Virginia, he was the first son of Presbyterian minister Joseph Ruggles Wilson and Janet Woodrow Wilson. He grew to maturity surrounded by people who took their religion seriously. His father was pastor of the First Presbyterian Church of Staunton, the most prominent pulpit in the Lexington Presbytery.[4] His ancestors on his mother's side included several generations of Presbyterian ministers.[5] Shortly after Woodrow's birth the family moved to Augusta, Georgia, where Joseph Wilson continued to advance within the Presbyterian Church. When Tommy, as he was then called, was four years old, the faction of Presbyterian Church[6] situated in the Confederate States of America held its first general assembly in the Augusta church and elected Reverend Wilson to the office of permanent clerk. He continued to hold high office in the Southern Church—including moderator, its highest office—until shortly before his death in 1903.[7] Joseph Wilson was the single greatest influence in his son's life.

Woodrow Wilson strove to hold an orthodox evangelical faith even as the changing times forced him to negotiate other views. He held Charles Hodge, his father's mentor and a chief defender of traditional American Calvinism at Princeton, in high regard.[8] The younger Wilson was impressed by Hodge's combination of intellectual strength and fidelity to the faith.[9] Academic inquiry was not an obstacle to Wilson's faith. On the contrary, he held contradiction explainable in mystery, drawing a distinction between the intellectual difficulties of faith and faith itself. In 1889 he confided in his journal that: "I saw the intellectual difficulties, but I was not *troubled* by them: they seemed to have no connection with my faith in the essentials of the religion I had been taught. Unorthodox in the reading of the standards of the faith, I am nevertheless orthodox in my faith."[10] Wilson remained securely within the Presbyterian tradition, but he was not what would later be termed *fundamentalist*.

The word *fundamentalist*, which came into the popular vocabulary following the publication, by two anonymous businessmen, of the *The Fundamentals* in 1910, is an inadequate word to describe the religious debates of Wilson's time period. It is inadequate to deal with the complexity of the issues the way Wilson's contemporaries at Princeton Seminary, A. A. Hodge (1823–1886) or Benjamin B. Warfield (1851–1921), dealt with them. These men, though theological conservatives, would have understood Wilson's support for the views of his uncle, James Woodrow, held on Theistic Darwinism. A. A. Hodge opened up accommodation to Darwin upon the death of his father Charles Hodge (1797–1878). While the elder Hodge, whom Wilson esteemed, had rejected Darwinism as atheistic, he left open the idea that the earth could change over time. In doing this he made clear that he had not totally rejected Darwin's observations, only the atheism that seemed to spring from the European reading of Darwin. His son continued this rejection of the materialistic approach to evolution but expanded upon the idea that the Bible accommodated the scientific findings of Darwin. These views were in turn expanded upon by Warfield, who took the ideas a step further and connected Darwin's theory of evolution to Calvin's doctrine of creation. To Warfield, Calvin clearly opened the door to the possibility of evolution as science was then presenting it. Warfield argued that Calvin's doctrine of creation was confined to two events, the creation of all *ex nihilo* and the creation of the human soul. All else was an ongoing act of providence. Thus science, when proven, was merely a revealing of providence in God's ongoing sustenance of creation.

These men, like Wilson, saw no religious conflict with academic inquiry into the origins of scripture or the universe, but maintained this did not pose a problem to faith in the Bible and providence. It is ironic, in light of later developments, that Warfield penned authoritative articles for both sides of the modernist fundamentalist debate. While writing his defense of evolution he was also penning an article for the first volume of *The Fundamentals* on the issue of the divinity of Christ. Following the fundamentalist movement in the early part of the twentieth century, this combination of beliefs became more difficult to maintain. But at Princeton, in Wilson's period, they rested somewhat comfortably together. A belief in Darwin did not equate with a rejection of scripture. Wilson was aware of this and robust in his defense of his uncle, James Woodrow, who lost his chair at Columbia Theological Seminary over teaching these ideas. But it is important to understand that this defense of his uncle's teachings did not require him to reject his faith in God or inspired scripture.[11]

Of greater importance to this study is that Wilson believed himself to be orthodox in his faith and that he took its patterns of reasoning seriously. That he took his faith seriously is shown by his statements on the Bible and divine providence. He understood more than the big themes of the faith in which he had been raised; he also noted the nuances of the theology that undergirded it. Occasionally in speeches he took time to show his audience that he understood their theological positions. In *Youth and Christian Progress*, Wilson commented with approval on the exclusion of a group of Unitarian ministers from the Inter-Church Conference on Federation:

> I spoke for a few moments with several gentlemen of those faiths which teach salvation by character. I regard such an enterprise as one of despair. . . . I would not want to offer [my character] as a certificate of my salvation. If I started out to make character I would be a prig. Character is a by product. If one sets out to make a by product by itself for itself he spoils the main product. . . . A church that pads itself with doctrine and thus betakes itself out of direct contact with the son of God is far less effective than a church that is in direct contact with Christ.[12]

While claiming to decry hidebound doctrine, he used the occasion to lay out the essential tenents of his evangelical faith. This passage, which Cooper has cited to document Wilson's alleged lack of interest in theology,[13] displays instead his grasp of his own theology, his understanding of the differences between Protestant denominations, and the shrewdness with which he could marshal that knowledge in his speeches.

These ideas and patterns of thought were so intermingled in Wilson that they made sacred and secular indistinguishable from each other. Critics of the idea that religious views significantly influenced Wilson point to the evident comfort with which he used nontheological political language. They note that he rejected the ministry when it would have been natural and consistent for him, if sincerely devoted to his religion, to follow the path of his father, his uncle, and so many of his Woodrow and Wilson forebears. This argument fails to take into account the degree to which his religion was at home in the world. Wilson's language and career, which today seem secular to modern historians, clothed the religious ideas that were his intellectual foundations. Theological ideas defined the essential character of the words he used and often the actions he took. The distinction between *secular* and *religious* that Cooper and many other modern historians attempt to make simply did not exist in Wilson's mind, as a young man, as a scholar, or as president of the United States.[14] Religion in secular garb was not unique to Wilson but common to the world he lived in. The Dutch leader Abraham Kuyper, also raised in a conservative Reformed tradition, derived similar political and social views from his faith as Wilson. Kuyper's 1898 "Stone Lectures," given at Princeton while Wilson was a professor, spelled these ideas out in great detail. The Dutch theologian, politician, and soon-to-be prime minister, said during that occasion that "America is destined in the providence of God to become the most glorious and noble nation the world has ever seen."[15] Wilson's theological and political framework follows Kuyper's pattern because it is a Calvinist/Reformed pattern. While the parallels are clear, they simply highlight the broad influence of the theological approach to politics that Wilson followed. There is no evidence of direct connection between Kuyper's views and Wilson's other than their shared theology. Though Wilson would have been very familiar with Kuyper's "Stone Lectures," we have no comment from Wilson.[16]

The Presbyterianism Woodrow inherited from his father was comfortable with the world. There was very little sacred/secular division in this theological outlook. The elder Wilson's sermons, like those of Calvin, Knox, or Edwards, were as likely to touch on business or statesmanship as a means to demonstrate Christian faith as they were to speak of the more *spiritual* matters that modern secular historians would recognize as religious. Thus it was natural for Woodrow to synthesize faith with what he believed to be his life mission: politics. In 1886 he explicitly compared the effective methods of politicians with those of preachers. The "success of great popular preachers contains a lesson for the students of politics. . . . " A political leader should follow the example of the great preachers by adapting their methods to politics, bypassing official channels, and identifying directly with constituents to win them to the cause.[17] Wilson sent the article in which he made this point to his father, who compared the recommendations of the article favorably to his own methods of theological inquiry. Joseph Wilson encouraged his son to adopt the same approach that he had used pursuing theological truth to his own inquiry into political truth.[18]

Wilson explicitly connected his theological tradition to his political life by portraying Calvinist theological thought and John Calvin himself in political terms in a set of Bryn Mawr College lecture notes prepared in 1887. To Professor Wilson, Calvin's theology was a political philosophy, and Calvin himself the "great reforming Christian *statesman*."[19] The future president referred to the Genevan reforms in political, social, and even literary terms, rather than theological ones. The praise which Wilson lavished upon Calvin on secular grounds reached the point where Wilson cited the *Institutes of the Christian Religion* as the cornerstone of French literature.[20]

That the young professor considered a foundational work of Protestant theology the cornerstone of literature in a Roman Catholic nation shows the future president's bias in favor of the Reformed faith, to say nothing of his parochial view of French history and culture. But these notes demonstrate the esteem with which he regarded Calvin's example as a statesman. Wilson believed that Geneva had produced a "government founded upon the authority of the congregation, centering in the church and the school, constituting as complete a fusion of church and state and as complete a subjection of the individual to humanity as ever existed in Greece or Rome." That government had international influence: "[French Calvinists'] participation in politics was an almost necessary outcome of their adherence to the faith of the great Christian statesman of Geneva: their work promised to be a reconstruction of the society as his had been."[21] Calvin's Geneva was ordered by a political theology with a specific imperative: to reconstruct the world on the pattern of God's covenant. To Wilson, though he had not yet fully formed his own political and international views,

Calvinist Christianity was inherently political and international in its mission. His Christian statesman was committed to social and political reform. That statesman must work to reconstruct his own society in covenantal patterns. If given the opportunity, he would reconstruct the world.

Wilson's views of Calvin were shared by his father. Two years before Woodrow's lectures at Bryn Mawr, the elder Wilson delivered an address to the Board of Directors of Southwestern Presbyterian Seminary. Father and son collaborated on this project, with Woodrow providing the outline and recommending content.[22] In the speech, Rev. Wilson described his own theology. He praised Zwingli, Knox, Huss, Latimer, and other Protestant reformers in general terms. When it came to Calvin and Calvin's Geneva, however, he devoted two printed pages to describing the reformer, his government, and his theology. Rev. Wilson compared Geneva with Nicene-era Alexandria and Calvin to Athanasius, the hero of the council of Nicea. He did not stop there:

> [Calvin's] Geneva[,] that modern but improved Athanasian Alexandria—the theology which fed the faith and fanned the hopes and fortified the courage of a "thus-saith-the-Lord" ancestry, the intelligence, the intrepidity, the inspiring activity of whose robust piety have never been excelled—the well-tried-theology which now signalizes our unequaled Catechisms and pre-eminent Confession[23] . . . the theology that has steadfastly refused to tolerate at the altar of a sin bearing sacrifice, any Priest; or on the throne of redeeming sovereignty, any King; or within the sanctuary of the Soul itself any Prophet—who shall shadow however dimly, or rival, however distantly, the all-sufficient Lord Jesus Christ. . . .[24]

Both the Bryn Mawr notes and his father's inaugural address present Calvin's form of government as more important than his explicitly theological doctrines. Participation in politics was a necessary, not an accidental, outcome of this Calvinist faith. The Christian politician acted from a faith in God and in accordance with an anticipation of the coming of a covenantal international world order. These principles were universal: Calvin's conception of order went beyond the church, to society and the world. A nineteenth- or twentieth-century Presbyterian statesman could demand no less of himself.

This theology was the root of Wilson's concept of order. His views on reform, progress, and revolution are found in the Presbyterian concepts of order and freedom. Freedom involved bringing chaos into order through obedience to God. Wilson's concept that "Obedience is Liberty" has made his views on government hard to categorize by those who have tried to label him as "progressive," "conservative," "Hamiltonian," or "Jeffersonian." The Presbyterian concepts of freedom and liberty were so intermingled with the ideas of law and order as to result in a unique category.[25]

As president of Princeton, Wilson evidenced these views and patterns from his religious background already seen in him as a young man and as a junior faculty member at Bryn Mawr. Students had hoped that the first layman president would suspend the requirement for compulsory chapel. While Wilson did suspend one Sunday afternoon service, he stiffened the chapel attendance requirements for the remaining services. When a group of students complained, requesting that chapel be made optional, he gave them a response consistent with his ideas on political liberty. "Why, gentlemen, it *is* optional. If you wish to go to chapel you may."[26] This was freedom in the Calvinist context of order. The students were free only to do the right thing. Biblical law instructed the believer how to live following salvation and set the pattern for organizing church, government, and community. In this order alone was true liberty. In a note to his confidential diary in 1889, Wilson wrote that freedom was being free to do right. It was freedom to respect authority and do right to the poor, it was a *law* of liberty. This doctrine that "obedience is liberty"[27] comes directly from Calvin's *Institutes*: "Obedience to the law of liberty is not only instructive, it brings the reward of freedom."[28]

In this theological-political system, obedience was primarily to the divine order administered through conscience. It superceded blind political obedience. Human institutions were inherently tainted with corruption. For this reason, Wilson generally did not trust human governments. The elect, with scripture, had the ability to instruct, and if necessary oppose, king as well as priest.[29] The individual Christian was accountable to God, the Bible, and conscience, before he or she was accountable to any human authority. The Holy Spirit and Scripture formed the conscience of the individual believer.[30] Human government that ordered itself by God's pattern should be obeyed, but the individual believer, accountable to God and conscience, had to bypass or disregard human authority if it resisted divine order. The mission and primary goal of all believers was to bring the world into liberty by means of God's covenantal order.

These views would have tremendous implications when Wilson became president and was faced with the challenge of chaotic international situations. Divinely charged in his own mind with bringing order, but limited by the inflexibility of national and international law, he fell back on these higher laws and reinterpreted human law to fit. Foreshadowing the frustration he would express to his colleagues at Versailles who argued there was a fixed and logical approach to international law, the young Wilson wrote: "Logic is no fact: it is thought given straight air lines, elevated above fact. Politics is made up of *relationships* and Law is the mirror of those relationships. . . . Law changes and so does liberty."[31]

Historian Harley Notter has commented on the importance with which the president invested the word *covenant*.[32] The word was in general use during the period and held other meanings to some who used it. To Wilson, however, the word "covenant" was the starting place for the integration of the sacred and the secular.[33] He embraced specific Southern Presbyterian terminology which was theological in nature but commonly applied by Presbyterians in a political context. The term *covenant*, derived from the Old Testament, reinforced by Paul's writings in the New Testament and redirected to focus on the whole earth rather than exclusively Israel, redefined during the Reformation, and fueled in its significance by the seventeenth-century Scottish Covenanters, was a word that held deep meaning to Wilson. The expression was widely used by both Princeton and Southern Presbyterian theologians.

Covenant theology delineated an interlinked relationship between the individual, church, society, government, and God. The idea of covenant organized an entire biblical hermeneutic.[34] God had set the world under his authority to operate within this system of legal covenants: God with man, God with creation, man with man. Obedience to these covenants would produce blessing, prosperity, peace, and was ultimately a sign of election by God for eternal salvation;

rebellion would produce the opposite. God ordered the universe, history, and his dealings with humankind through these interconnected covenants. Human beings were either *blessed* or *cursed* based upon their adherence. Leaders chosen by God must understand this covenantal plan. They were responsible for leading the people into this better world order.

Wilson grew up with this idea that God ordered the universe.[35] Though the world had fallen short of that divine order, God's will would, nonetheless, bring the world to conformity in time through the mediation of Christ, the work of the Holy Spirit, and the righteous actions of the elect. Bringing the world into a covenantal pattern was, to Wilson, the purpose that directed all of human history. Though opposed by evil, this order would ultimately prevail. This eschatology defined Wilson's politics, particularly his ideas of *progress* and *reform*. It also caused him to divide people into two camps. A person served either the good purposes of God or the evil opposition to those purposes.

The influence of covenantal theology on the future president was not limited to the general ideas common among Southern and Princeton Presbyterians. Wilson's father explicitly organized his theology and his politics around the idea of the covenant.[36] He preached the fixed order of God's universe and the covenantal order of redemption.[37] To Joseph Wilson, covenant explained social order, gender rules, racial and class positioning, and human responsibility. Covenant explained how things ought to be in light of God's sovereignty. Both Joseph and Woodrow used this word with theological and political meaning simultaneously. They shared a natural mental progression from the idea of a covenant of the elect, to a national covenant, to an international covenant.

Though father and son saw the terms of the covenant as clear and absolute, another aspect of Presbyterian Calvinist theology complicated this clarity: the principle of *antinomy*. Scripture was by definition infallible and could not be contradictory. Antinomy, or as some called it, *concursus,* made sense of the seeming contradictions of scripture by attributing them to the limitation of human understanding. As a respected Calvinist theologian explained this concept: "The whole point of an antinomy . . . is that it is not a real contradiction, though it looks like one. It is an *apparent* incompatibility between two truths."[38] The modernist approach to religion was to make the mystery and miracles of the Bible explainable by materialism and science; the fundamentalist approach reduced religion to what the Wilsons considered a facile, anti-intellectual leap of faith. Their form of Presbyterianism taught them to accept that truths could still be valid while maintaining some manner of tension with each other. The appearance of contradiction, in foreign policy or in theology, merely pointed to a truth that required the simultaneous holding of both points of view.[39] It was a "living" truth which required the believer to grasp its "spirit."[40]

Reverend Wilson passed on this pattern of thinking to his son. He, like his Calvinist contemporaries, grasped the essential theological antinomy upon which their system was founded, the conflict between human free will and God's sovereign election. He asserted that a believer must follow these two seemingly incompatible truths, human responsibility and divine predestination, but need not reconcile them, only believe them.[41] This basic intellectual tension provided a cornerstone that allowed other apparently contradictory ideas to be accommodated.

Once embraced, antinomy did not confine itself merely to the sphere of religion. Joseph Wilson applied it to the workings of God in society. Believing that providence ordered the affairs of men, he was forced to grapple with the terrible contradictions to providence that he saw in the great tragedies that had engulfed southern society following the Civil War. In sermons, he explained the apparent failure of God's providence to his congregation as a failure of human ability to understand God's purposes:

> However God may sometimes appear to have forgotten you. This which troubles you is nothing more than an appearance. Providences are often seemingly adverse, as you for the moment and in piecemeal look at them, but they are never really adverse.[42]

Scripture and providence could not fail, though it might appear so. The real failure was flawed and limited humanity's inability to comprehend God's ultimate unified purpose.

Antinomy turned the strict legal sense of covenant into an order of the heart. Belief in a good God required a continued obedience to that good purpose regardless of the apparent circumstances. It became a spiritual, not a human legal, structure. It owed ultimate allegiance only to the moral authority of God himself. It created an inner sense of order that often compelled Wilson when president to act upon his sense of duty to God and then find a legal rationale for his action later. The act undertaken in obedience toward God was concurrent with human law but superceded it.

The personal sense of obedience to God tended to further personalize issues of law and organization for Wilson. Private channels which were organic and relational and which bypassed legal structures appealed to him. He could honor his allegiance to God and fulfill the "spirit of the law," while avoiding the complications that the facts of the law as others interpreted it presented. And he could do so with confidence in his heart that he was never in violation of the law. Following the philosophy he held on orthodoxy to the faith ("[un]orthodox in [his] reading of the standards of the faith," but "orthodox in [his] faith") it seems that Wilson was unorthodox in his reading of the standards of the law yet, in his heart, orthodox in his obedience to the law. This pattern of thought toward political matters created difficulties. Contemporaries often saw in him inconsistency, or worse, hypocrisy. He, on the other hand, remained certain that he acted from a single set of principles. Logically contradictory ideas coexisted comfortably in his mind, balanced in a tension that he accepted as God's will. This synthesis is implied in the line from his talk on political liberty: "Logic is no fact: it is thought given straight air lines, elevated above fact."[43]

Antinomy created an inner, personal, and subjective picture of truth in Wilson's mind. To a thinking Calvinist believer wrestling with theological antinomy in the conflict between justice and mercy, for example, the intellectual balance that the person finally arrived at, the point that seemed to be the appropriate point of truthful tension between the two, determined whether the action that person took in a given situation was to call for punishment or forgiveness. This does not mean that the individual would have recognized that he or she was acting subjectively. Holding this truth, though it might be personal and subjective, would seem to be a necessity that should be as clear to others as it was in the believer's own mind. Since the scripture and historic creeds had spelled out the principles that were in tension, and since others within the Presbyterian church generally agreed upon those principles, the subjective point of balance between the two seemed to be self-evident.[44] This mystery was something Presbyterians assumed themselves to have agreed upon. When Wilson was fully engaged with conflicting points of view, physically and emotionally well, he would often use this pattern of analysis to compromise or add another perspective to his thinking process. In doing so he remained fully convinced that he was acting in accordance with *principle*. When he was in crisis, or ill, and kept away from intellectual complications, he often became intransigent and morally simplistic, citing that same principle as his justification.

Wilson's antinomy in his approach to principle was a mystery at times to those who worked with him. He conveyed the impression to some, like Keynes, that the truth he was committed to was beyond human language or human ability to express fully. Yet he seemed completely clear in his own mind about how these contradictions were held together. Wilson negotiated the difficulties of his faith with the confident assurance of his own inner clarity, as Charles Thompson would later observe during the Mexican crisis.[45] Puzzled that others had difficulty finding this clarity, he commented, "I am capable, it would seem, of being satisfied spiritually without being satisfied intellectually."[46] Yet this was not altogether true; Wilson was often intellectually satisfied with mystery. His understanding of Calvinist antinomy allowed him to move between disparate thoughts with a confidence that they were not really inconsistent. Despite this mystery the principles remained clear to him in their essentials. One needed only to do one's duty, be faithful, work hard for divine principles and all would work out as God intended. That was all the intellectual satisfaction he needed in the end.

Antinomy in thought, when combined with a belief in divine providence, effectively elevated the opinions of the believer to the significance of divine utterance. This resulted because the person could not always divide in his or her mind between divine and human. The equation of personal opinion with divine decree would not have been conscious to Wilson and many of his coreligionists. Indeed the thought of doing so would have been blasphemous to them. It was, however, the way they treated their opinions when challenged. If forced to fight, they would defend their principles as if they were the revealed word of God, rejecting compromise or alternatives as not only immoral, but heretical.

Wilson's Presbyterian tradition placed a higher importance on the word of God than on the institution. The word produced institutions such as the church that, if they embodied that word, existed to serve it. The essential word, of course, was Christ himself revealed in the written word of God. But to a lesser degree it was the word spoken by a leader or preacher inspired by that word. Sunday preaching among American evangelicals had developed into a fine art. The importance placed upon the word also included written contracts or covenants between people. An examination of the constitutions and books of church order demonstrates that the Covenanter tradition, and a high regard for covenants in general, was woven into the very fabric of Presbyterian organization and structure. In his youth Wilson spent much time writing constitutions and attempting to bring order to his life through covenants. As a young man he formed "a solemn covenant" with his friend Charlie Talcott that they would school all their powers and passions for the work of establishing the principles they held in common.[47] Wilson took this high regard for the word and applied it to words in general. His article "Mere Literature," published in the *Atlantic* in 1893, articulated a religious view of language regarding literature in general even as others, according to Wilson, disparaged it as "mere literature."[48]

Language was vital because the intuitive nature of the covenant required a messenger/leader to explain and establish it. Wilson had been taught from infancy about the divine messengers of the Bible: Moses, the prophets, and the ultimate messenger, Jesus Christ. His childhood was filled with stories of the Reformed heroes of the past: Luther, Calvin, Zwingli, Jonathan Edwards. In addition, growing up in the South, he heard the stories of great Christian leaders of Virginia such as Thomas "Stonewall" Jackson and Robert E. Lee. Finally, the very structure of the church in which Wilson grew up required an inspired leader who could motivate a group of elders and get his vision enacted while still adhering to the Presbyterian form of constitutional government.

The emphasis on the need for a divinely inspired leader to speak a visionary word to the institution set up another antinomy in Wilson's mind between the individual and the organization. Though order within the organization must always be maintained, a divine messenger, as an individual, must emerge preeminent to make that order fully functional. This was the function of the Holy Spirit in Trinitarian theology. The Holy Spirit at the right time inspired or *gifted* the right persons to lead the institutions they were called to lead. The inspired leader supported by a loyal constitutional body was the ideal method for bringing God's covenantal order to earth. Believing that he was a divinely called leader provided an outlet for action that relieved the intellectual tension set up by the antinomy of his inner thinking process.[49]

Wilson studied debate as an undergraduate at Princeton. He worked hard at developing his rhetorical and writing skills in order to strengthen his ability to be that leader with the inspiring word. For Wilson, words themselves were the means of establishing covenantal order. To do God's will, to lead people or nations, the statesman used language. Rhetoric and the power of persuasion were paramount. He was the ultimate preacher and must "actively advocate truth." The "statesman must possess an orator's soul, an orator's words, an orator's action. To nobleness of thought he must add nobleness of word and conduct."[50] The New Testament principle of the "word made flesh" is evident in Wilson. The word was embodied in a man. A great orator, a prophet, a preacher to the nations is what a statesman should be. To Wilson, words not only *had* substance, they *were* substance. They created reality. It takes little imagination to realize that this faith in words would become even more powerful when as president those words created policy.

Wilson's early writing focused on this idea of the great man or divine leader. Images including statesman, prophet, and soldier appear in the first set of articles that Wilson wrote, at age nineteen, published in his father's newspaper, the Wilmington *North Carolina Presbyterian*. From August 11, 1876, until January 30, 1877, the younger Wilson wrote seven articles and one speech, "The Ideal Statesman." These early essays illuminate the way in which he perceived the world, religion, and God. They also show the early views that he held of

his personal mission in life. Emerging from the cocoon of his religious childhood these writings stand as a testimony to his thought
as he entered adulthood. Though Wilson added to and complicated
the ideas expressed in these early writings, they are important to any
understanding of the adult Wilson. He never abandoned this basic
view of the world which he had developed in childhood. In a crisis
he would often return to the simpler language of the good versus evil
morality of these first articles.

These writings show that whatever dualism Wilson had inherited
by way of Calvinist antinomy, he did not embrace the *sacred vs. secular*
divide of pietist Christianity. His faith was fully engaged with human
culture. The essay "Work-Day Religion," published August 11, 1876,
attacked those who reserved their religion for holy times and places.
Wilson challenged his readers to make no separation in life between
the Sabbath and the rest of the week. True religion was a "religion per-
vading every act—which is carried with us into every walk of life and
made our one stay and hope."[51] Religion was holistic; it was an all-of-
life, every day, affair. It was also a great battle in which the righteous
would ultimately prevail.

The following week he wrote a second article, "Christ's Army."
It spoke of this hard-fought battle in the world in which the forces
of evil, though great, would "quail before the uplifted swords of the
Spirit." This battle would be a steady progress for the people of God:
"the army of saints ever gains ground under divine generalship; now
slowly, now rapidly, driving before them with irresistible force the
broken ranks of the enemy." There was no place for compromise on
principle. "For there is no middle course, no neutrality. Each one must
enlist either with the followers of Christ or those of Satan." Though
the truth may be an intellectual antinomy, it was still truth and any
resistance to its "principle" was opposition, not just to the idea of
truth, but to Christ himself.[52]

This view is a product of the world that nurtured Wilson. One of
his father's more famous sermons states:

> Whatever God says is to them absolute truth; whatever God com-
> mands is to them absolute duty; whatever God covenants to give, is to
> them absolute certainty. His word is to them the end of all controversy.
> His will the end of all authority: His honor the end of all desire: His

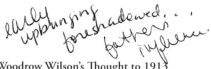

holiness the end of all living: His beauty the end of all search. They believe Him more than they do their closest friend, more than they believe themselves, more.[53]

These writings foreshadow the adult Wilson, unable to compromise with anyone who stood in the way of good as he perceived it. The thinking of the man who would battle the trustees at Princeton in 1907 over the location of the Graduate School and drive himself to the breaking point campaigning against the Senate reservationists more than a decade later is already present in the nearly twenty-year-old of 1876.

Wilson clearly believed he had been called to lead this army, as a messenger of Christ. The specific wording of "Christ's Army" demonstrates how the youthful Wilson hoped to accomplish his mission. The term *sword of the Spirit* comes from the book of Ephesians, where the sword symbolized the word of God.[54] The word of God was the weapon of the messenger. The Apostle Paul instructed his readers to pray for his boldness as he delivered the message as a good warrior/ambassador on his way to Rome in chains. While the Bible recognized only one sword of the Spirit, the word of God, Wilson pluralized and individualized this idea. The focus of his article was on the heroic human messengers inspired by the Spirit, rather than the one historic divine message. This pattern became increasingly significant as he matured and developed a larger understanding of his own calling as the messenger.

"A Christian Statesman" followed the two earlier essays. Not quite twenty years old, Wilson was already looking to politics as the way of expressing his commitment to the divine call. His father's influence at this point in his life is evident. Joseph Wilson, like many preachers, repeated his better sermons multiple times over the years. One, which Woodrow would have grown up hearing, encouraged believers to serve as God's messenger in many professions. Foremost of the professions he listed was that of statesman.

> These who lift their eyes to the city Abraham saw which alone hath foundations and who stretch their arms towards the conqueror's crown Paul touched! An common ordinary believer, what is he? Well, he is a statesman who believes in the testimony of history, and he shapes national policies in accordance with the teachings of the past.[55]

Another sermon preached several times, once at Wilmington just two years before the publication of Wilson's article, would have been a direct encouragement to the seventeen-year-old son sitting before him in the pew. The sermon touched upon the issue of the sonship of all believers to God:

> Our present sonship, however, bears it would seem, but a faint *resemblance* to that which is future. / And in *this* obvious sense it is that "it doth not yet appear what we shall be." The grain of corn you cast into the ground. Would you ever dream of the grand stock . . . which shall spring up from the little grain. . . . Or, the feeble infant, laying helpless in its mother's arms; could you imagine . . . that it is ever to strengthen into the broad-shouldered, large-minded man, by whose enterprise a nation is to be enriched, or upon whose statesmanship it is to depend for its security and its glory? Moses in the bulrushes—who could have foreseen in that babe the Moses of Sinai and the wilderness? Small are all human *beginnings*; in these beginnings is found only the obscurest prophecy.[56]

Nurtured upon this diet of hope in the possibility of becoming God's messenger, perhaps a statesman–savior like Moses, Wilson made his pact with Charlie Talcott. He recounted several years later in a letter to his future wife, Ellen Axson, that he "had then, as I still have, a very earnest political creed and very pronounced political ambitions." To this end he and Talcott had formed this "solemn covenant" that they would school all their powers and passions for the work of establishing the principles they held in common. The letter goes on, in biblical language, to describe this pivotal event in his life. Like the Hebrew sons of Issachar[57] he was determined to "know the times into which he has been born."[58] For those who hold that Wilson was only vaguely aware of theological concepts, passages like this one are difficult to explain. The twenty-year-old Wilson used obscure biblical passages, which he was familiar with, in casual letters to friends, in this case his future wife.

Wilson wrote "A Christian Statesman" during this time of great decision in his life. This series of articles show that he had developed a comprehensive worldview and a defined purpose for his life. He would be a Christian statesman, a great national leader, a messenger of God, a modern day Moses. At the same time as he was producing these articles he also worked on a speech, "The Ideal Statesman," which appeared in Wilson's private notebook in April 1875 and was delivered as a speech in January 1877. Together these two works show not only that Wilson saw his calling as that of a statesman but also how he intertwined his father's idea of mission and the Calvinist world view with his own concept of what that statesman should be. The phrasing he used is a reflection of his father's: ". . . he does the deeds of the present in the declining light of the past not only but in the rising dawn of the future as well."[59]

This phrasing—using the past to work out the present and future—may have helped justify his study of history as a way to a statesman's career. In 1885 he wrote in a letter that his strength was the ability to interpret the past into the practical life of the present and thereby impel people by this methodology to achieve great things. To this end he was ready to accept the providential ordering of his life.[60] The statesman was to be "prophetic," his "faith is to be in Christ his Saviour," his truth was to be "in accordance with the Bible's standard." He was to strive for perfection and "work and trust in God."[61]

Bringing God's covenantal order was the task at hand. Despite the complications and intuitive nature of truth, the statesman must stay with the truth and "earnestly seek aid from God, who will surely hold him responsible for the course he pursues."[62] God's truth and God's order, not mere political advantage, motivated the Christian statesman. This sense of having to give an account to God reinforced his inability to compromise. Logical or intuitive, truth was truth. The Christian statesman was above partisan politics. That his position and his principles could be considered *partisan* by others of good will was not addressed in Wilson's writings, as a youth or at any other period of his life. Truth was fixed and must be found and obeyed. Unlike law or contracts, it did not evolve or change with time. The divine messenger must be clear about the truth. The statesman/messenger must come down from the mountain with the course set on tablets of stone and lead the people to the promised land. He could not afford to compromise principle for he would have to give an account.

Keynes, who observed Wilson later during the Versailles negotiations, said that the president had only words with no "flesh of life" to clothe the "commandments he had thundered from the White House."[63] What Keynes did not grasp was that to Wilson the words were the flesh of life. The future president emerged from his teens with a deep conviction that he was to be a Christian statesman. He clung fixedly to this conviction throughout his life, even at the height of his academic career. Politics and religion united in Wilson with no more tension than any of his other Presbyterian antinomies. He perceived his spiritual life as at its height during the periods when he felt the call to politics most strongly.[64]

Organization, including government, was the other side of a Presbyterian dialectic between the divine messenger and the regard for order. Wilson's apparent intellectual conflict between the individual and the organization has at times baffled scholars as much as it did his contemporaries. Historian Henry May argued that Wilson's politics shifted suddenly from conservative individualism to collective progressivism between 1909 and 1914, and that his religious opinions changed as well.[65] Apart from May's contested uses for *conservative* and *progressive*, this argument fails to allow for the president's thinking patterns. May accurately documents differing aspects of Wilson's thought but fails to note that these apparent conflicts were evident in his thought throughout his career. In Wilson's mind these individualist and collectivist ideas about social reform coexisted as peacefully as election and free will.

As an evangelical Protestant Woodrow Wilson gave the task priority over the organization in religious matters. This certainly did not mean that the organization, in Wilson's case the Presbyterian church, was unimportant. What it did mean for evangelicals was that the task of discipling the nations and delivering the message of the gospel (the Great Commission) preceded and superceded the organization of the church. Protestants had been ready to form new organizations when they felt the existing church structure was impeding the task. Wilson took these religious priorities and adapted them to his political task.[66]

Two speeches in 1909 illuminate the future president's antinomy between the corporate task which the organization was to serve and the individual messenger who would motivate the organization to fulfill that task. He addressed McCormick Theological Seminary in November on "The Ministry and the Individual." In this speech he appears to argue that the individual superceded the organization. The

Divine messenger

ministry has only one responsibility, he maintained, the message of salvation. That message was for individuals. Society was saved one person at a time. He celebrated the heroic individual standing against collective society and its institutions. This speech described the divine messenger as Wilson understood it.[67]

A little more than five months earlier, however, on May 26, he had delivered an anniversary address to the Hartford Theological Seminary. Its title was "The Present Task of the Ministry," and it called just as eloquently for collective social responsibility. The individual was part of a greater plan and must commit himself to the betterment of the world for the good of all. The mission of Christianity was to save the whole world. The individual was only a part of this great collective mission. Even personal salvation was only part of the process through which the entire world was to be saved.[68] This speech focused on the other side of the antinomy, the great collective covenantal order that the individual was responsible to assist in bringing about through the church.

May cites the November speech as evidence of Wilson's nonprogressive, nonsocial approach to religion and social issues. What emerges from a comparison of the two speeches, however, is that Wilson held both ideas simultaneously and saw no contradiction between them. In November, he referred to his May 26 speech without any indication that it represented a change in his thinking. He reconciled May's apparent contradiction by holding the organization and the individual in antinomy. God's covenants integrated the roles of church, government, and individual into an interconnected set of relationships. Men could try to understand these matters rationally. They would at times succeed. A lack of understanding, however, could not excuse disobedience to the covenant by either individuals or organizations.

Covenantal order implemented through the empowered words of an inspired messenger was the task, superceding human organization. The individual was responsible for giving himself or herself to the task. The business of the Christian church and minister was to show men their relation "to the great world processes."[69] The task was a corporate one in which the individual was subject to the greater purpose, and for this reason creating organizations was necessary. Nevertheless, when the organization was given too great a priority Wilson took a different line of argument. "[No] *organization* can be said to love the person

Sometimes rational worked but it didn't

and example of Christ."[70] No organization can take responsibility. No organization was any better than the individuals within it. There was no promise of vitality in the church without the individual. Collective action was necessary and appropriate for some "temporal purposes," such as social reform, or reformation of the international order, but the message and task of Christianity must remain individualistic.[71] No organization could be a divine messenger. The messenger had to be an individual, a Moses, a Calvin, a Gladstone, . . . or a Wilson. He shifted between these two idealistic frameworks with no apparent realization of, or discomfort with, their contradictory nature, because he saw no contradiction in them.

In a set of lecture notes from 1894 Wilson laid out further boundaries that he placed on both individualism and state organization. The three lectures, collectively titled *The Nature of the State and its Relation to Progress,* begin with the statement, "A State is a people independently organized for law within a definite territory." Thus the state as an organization began with *a people.* He defined *law* as the general will of the people, given shape by the church and religion along with other factors. The individual was essential to a functioning state and yet the state called that individual, as an individual, to something more. He described the state itself in religious terminology: "the eternal, natural embodiment and expression of a higher life than the individual." This collective of individuals, made one by their adherence to this "higher life," was provided with a set of vehicles for progress: struggle (self-discipline), religion, and education. These vehicles created an interaction between individuals and the expression of higher life, the state, to which they had given themselves. That interaction promoted progress. The executive in the state was an elected father figure, or guide. Though this interaction could be unpredictable it was not chaotic in the properly functioning state, for "liberty is found only where there is the best order." Progress of the state, in Wilson's view, was a series of dialectics that resulted in an almost Hegelian pattern within history. This progress in a properly run state was accomplished with the fluid ease of providential antinomy working in the contradictions between state, society, and the individual to produce a better world order.[72]

Wilson spelled out further the tension in which he held organization and individual in an article which he wrote at age twenty-three.

This article, "Self Government in France," dated September 1879, took a negative view toward governments and organizations when they existed as an end in themselves. While Wilson complimented the noble aims of the French Revolution, he argued that its original leaders, as well as the subsequent leaders of France, thwarted those aims. They would continue to do so until the French could rid themselves of their tendency toward centralized government. France would careen between despotism and disorder because the individuals who made up French society were incapable of moderate constitutional action. "The French mind seems to run at right angles to the law, and parallel with every dangerous extreme."[73]

This tendency was, in part, due to the French Catholic inability to hold contradiction in tension. In yet another set of lecture notes, Wilson praised Edmund Burke and defended him against those critics who accused him of inconsistency for opposing the underlying principles of the French Revolution. Burke was not inconsistent but merely holding a proper antinomy in his mind. Wilson argued that Burke was the champion of orderly reform. Such reform was only possible by holding contradiction together as one. "All government, indeed every human benefit and enjoyment, every virtue and every prudent act, is founded on compromise and barter. We balance inconveniences: We give and take; we remit some rights that we may enjoy others. . . ." To Wilson, Burke was consistent. He appeared inconsistent to others because he held a broader understanding of truth, an understanding that included the contradictory patterns that Wilson grasped intuitively.

Continuing to spell out the reason why the dialectic between the individual and the organization broke down in France, Wilson argued that the failure of the French government was due to a flaw in the mind of the *individual* French citizen, who was seemingly unable to comprehend that the state is to be the servant of the individual. "Thus were even the imaginations of the most hopeful reformers enslaved by a pernicious idea of the functions of the state. To recognize in a government only the agent or instrument of the governed would have been to them as impossible as to efface all the past history of France. To them the state *was* the nation." He decried the elimination of the divine messenger by an organization, in this case the Roman Catholic church. Wilson argued that a large part of the social problem in France was due to the role of the church. It had conditioned the French to place too high a regard on the organization and too low a regard on the individual. This failure to keep the proper priority between organization and individual produced a society that vacillated between violent revolution and passivity in the face of tyranny.[74]

In Wilson's understanding of covenantal order the Pope could not be a divine messenger because of the structure of the Roman Catholic church. To some degree, of course, this opinion represented his Protestant prejudice against the Roman church. Of greater specific importance to Wilson's thoughts about leadership, however, was the fact that the Pope derived his authority from an *organization* and not from the *people* through divinely appointed constitutional (covenantal) means. The Roman church did away with the dialectic between the task and the individual and replaced it with church hierarchy. Papal authority was derived from this hierarchy, an organization that Wilson believed superceded individual conscience and existed apart from the task. In a later criticism of Roman Catholicism he argued explicitly that its "organization" diminished the need for preaching, a practice which was essential to his understanding of the messenger's function.[75]

In a series of letters to the *North Carolina Presbyterian* responding to a set of moderately pro-Catholic articles in the local paper, Wilson did not blame theology but organization as the flaw of the Roman church. He pointed to education as the gate by which this organization made headway into American society. The Roman Catholic church was "openly antagonistic to the principles of free government."[76] These attacks were moderated with a note that they were not directed at *individual* Catholics, who could be good citizens, but at the *organization* of the Roman Church.

In later years Wilson would compliment individual members of the Catholic clergy who did good for humanity and benefited society.[77] He could be very loyal to individual Catholics whom he considered friends. When his friend Colonel E. M. House and Secretary of the Treasury (and son-in-law) William Gibbs McAdoo approached the president with their suspicions that his secretary, Joseph Tumulty, might be controlling the information that reached the oval office in order to aid Roman Catholic political interests, he dismissed their accusations out of hand. House noted that the president was unwavering in his loyalty to Tumulty.[78] Yet over the next month Wilson and House privately discussed ways to "strike the Catholics a public blow."[79] He had no problem expressing loyalty and friendship to individual Catholics, even when their Catholicism was the issue. Nevertheless, there was always an undercurrent of suspicion toward the institution and leadership of the Catholic church. Wilson had no difficulty with the use of authority. But he believed that the world would be a much better place if run by a constitutional system of authority that could maintain the proper priority between the individual and the organization.

Wilson's conflicting approaches to social issues, his personal style of administration, and his seemingly contradictory ideals reflected his religious thought applied to political life and society. The individual versus the collective is but one set of *truths* which Wilson kept in internal tension. Recognizing that he gave priority to the task (in his tradition, God's message and the consequences produced by that message) over the organization helps to explain some of his actions while in the White House. For the task of reforming the international order and bringing world peace he could envision great organizations: a League of Nations, at times a world court, nations bound in solemn covenants. These were all organizations of individuals (or, in the League of Nations, individual sovereign nations) bound together in a voluntary covenant to further the task of world peace. When he perceived organizations to exist apart from the task, such as his own State Department (and at times the apparatus of the federal government in general), Wilson would bypass them and use individuals such as House or Tumulty to further the mission. He was, after all, the messenger. He held legitimate authority from God through the people via a covenantal/constitutional process. Opposition to him was opposition to God's order. This opposition would need to be defeated either by direct confrontation or by bypassing it altogether. In a crisis he would bypass opponents and their legal arguments and appeal directly to the people from whom he, through the will of providence, derived his authority. He sustained an almost absolute faith that if he could speak to people they would understand and agree. The word of the messenger carried within it the power to create a providential order in the minds of the people.

Wilson believed the United States was divinely chosen to do God's will on earth. This allowed him to blend even more seamlessly the central elements of his faith with those of his mission in politics. A divinely ordained body must support the messenger. For spiritual purposes that body was the church, for political purposes that body was God's other minister: the state.[80] That state was obviously the United States. This idea was not unique to Wilson. Beginning with the Puritans, expressly spelled out by Jonathan Edwards, and continuing throughout the nineteenth century, the idea of America as God's chosen nation gained strength. A strongly postmillennial eschatology fueled a belief in progress, supported this view, and looked forward to the ultimate triumph of a peaceful, earthly expression of the kingdom of God. The "reign of God" was not a material theocracy but a spiritual kingdom set up in the collective minds of Christian people and given expression among the nations of the world by behavior consistent with the rule of Christ.[81] Human governments run by people who had themselves submitted to the reign of Christ would administer this "kingdom" through humanly created institutions. As a result, the institutions themselves would be transformed into divinely chosen vehicles that God could use for his purpose. American adherents to this view saw the United States as the chosen instrument to bring this order about.

A desire among Americans to see purpose in the bloody carnage of the American Civil War led to a belief that this event had purified the nation in fire and blood for a chosen task. Though Wilson was a southerner and continued to support many southern positions such as states rights and limited federal government, he was not obsessed with the "lost cause."[82] He saw the outcome of the war as providence preparing a great country to serve God's purposes among the nations of the world.[83] This version of American Christian postmillennialism fit well with what Wilson believed about himself and his calling as a messenger statesman. These views were essential if he were to sustain the synthesis between his sense of divine calling and its expression in secular politics. But once entered into these views made the task simple and clear. God planned to bring his order to the earth. America was God's chosen nation and he the chosen leader following his election. Once he became president it would be a simple matter of seeing what moments and opportunities God opened for him to bring that order to the nation and the world.

Some historians have argued that Wilson had no systematic plan of international relations until the events of the First World War thrust the United States onto the international stage. It is true that Wilson had propounded few specifics regarding international relations before becoming president. Given that, however, his theological mindset infused him with an ideal of what the world should look like and what America's role should be in that world. In an early campaign speech during his run for president he spelled these views out quite clearly:

> There is a spirit that rules us. If I did not believe in Providence I would feel like a man going blindfolded through a haphazard world. I do believe in Providence. I believe that God presided over the inception of this nation; I believe that God planted in us the visions of liberty; I believe that men are emancipated in proportion as they lift themselves to the conception of Providence and of divine destiny, and therefore I cannot be deprived of the hope that is in me—in the hope not only that concerns myself, but the confident hope that concerns the nation—that we are chosen and prominently chosen to show the way to the nations of the world how they shall walk in the paths of liberty.
>
> How great a destiny it is and how small those who intrigue against providence. How God must laugh! I do not know his ways; I do not know by what method he will work the great plot out; but I do know that there is a power whose approaching breath we can feel, that is going to purify the whole air of American politics, chasten every selfish man, drive out every corrupt purpose, bring on the morning with its light, and as the day broadens men shall look about them and say, "Behold the heavens are clear again! God's sun is in the heavens and all shall be right."[84]

This speech, rife with biblical imagery and contemporary millennial allusions, was the product of a steadily growing conviction of America's place in the world and of his place of leadership in America.

In one of Wilson's stock speeches, "Leaders of Men," delivered at various locations from 1889 until 1900, he expands upon the idea of the universal application of the moral law of God. Highlighting the way in which he applied his theological views to his vision of America and leadership overall, he quotes from both the King James Bible and the evangelical minister of the Presbyterian church that he was a member of while teaching at Wesleyan. He applies his religious understanding of God's moral law to the idea of national and international leadership. "Moral law was not written for men alone . . . it was written as well for nations, and for nations great as this of which we are citizens. If nations reject and deride that moral law, there is a penalty which will inevitably follow." He refered to Otto von Bismarck, the Prussian statesman, as a "divine hedge" around German Kaiser Wilhelm II. The Kaiser's dismissal of the Chancellor had removed that "hedge." Speaking of the function of the presidential office that Theodore Roosevelt would later describe as the "bully pulpit," Wilson argued that the statesman is the mouthpiece, the minister of the nation he serves who must arouse the awareness of the community of itself.[85] He must make the nation aware of its destiny. For a Calvinist like Wilson to be God's messenger, he would have to be a statesman in a divinely predestined nation. Borrowing spiritual terminology regarding the nature of the reign spelled out by the millennial views of the day, he argued that the self-awareness of its destiny created in the nation by the Christian statesman would develop an internal rule without adding more government or laws.[86] It would express itself in the hearts of the people of the nation at the right time. Leaders and reformers appear providentially at the right time. England and Germany became Protestant because their leaders came at the right time. America would have its leaders at the right time as well. The proclamation of truth to the nation at the right time in its history by the right messenger would create a society formed around an *idea*, indeed around a *word*. That society would then become a reflection of the perfect law written on the hearts of men, a type of "New Covenant" in the Christian sense.[87]

This concern for the right time, which he sometimes referred to as "Providential timing," was a consistent theme of Wilson throughout his life. In a letter dated February 1885 he wrote that he wanted to contribute something substantial to the political knowledge of the country. To do so he felt the need to stand apart, at the present, from radical measures that the country was not yet ready for so that he could act more forcefully when the time was right. Acting too early would discredit him and destroy his chances of being listened to when his time arrived.[88] This did not, however, preclude the possibility of more radical action when the time was right.

What society needed was not more law but a change in the character, the hearts, of the nation. According to Tumulty and others who spoke with the president, his veto of the Volstead Act and opposition to the XVIII Amendment instituting Prohibition was on precisely these grounds. Alcohol abuse was a problem of the heart, over which the government had no jurisdiction. The only law that could be effective on this problem was spiritual. The government could only implement it through moral persuasion and a societal change of heart.[89]

On Wilson's birthday in 1889, in the same month he first gave the speech "Leaders of Men," he confided in his personal diary "I have great confidence in progress; I feel the movement that is in the affairs and am conscious of a persistent push behind the present order." He anguished over the length of time it was taking to prepare him for his life task. He spoke of himself, using the biblical terminology regarding the sons of Issachar, as a man with an ability to "interpret the times." The birthday entry finishes with the plea "Why may not the present age write through me, its political autobiography?"[90]

In "The Ideals of America," an address written twelve years later, he described the United States as the "instructor of the world" and argued that "it was plain destiny that we should come to this." He then predicted that the coming century "shall see us a great power in the world." Perhaps alert to his political autobiography he wrote "Let us put our leading characters at the front; let us pray that vision may come with power; let us ponder our duties . . . like men who seek to serve, not subdue the world; . . . and bring a great age in with the coming of our day of strength."[91]

A little more than six months later, on July 4, 1902, Wilson blended even further the ideas of his religion and political life in a speech titled "Religion and Patriotism." It was clear in this speech that he saw patriotism in America as synonymous with obedience to the law of God. Patriotism was a covenantal duty that the Christian in the United States was bound to perform. He felt that he need not encourage patriotism in America, but merely remind people what it means to be servants of God and they would automatically serve their country. Being a good servant of God was inextricably intertwined with being a good American.[92]

Wilson's bedrock conviction that God had destined the United States to instruct and lead the world was further evidenced by other writings. His multivolume *A History of the American People* ends with the words: "Statesman knew that it was to be their task to release the energies of the country for the great day of trade and manufacture which was to change the face of the world. . . ."[93] On February 23, 1903, he again used the "redeemer nation" language: "There is nothing that gives a man more profound belief in providence than the history of this country. It is undoubtably a Providential system."[94] Two and a half years later he spoke even more explicitly of the task of the nation in relationship to the world. "There is a mighty task before us and it welds us together. It is to make the United States a mighty Christian nation, and to Christianize the world."[95] Continuing the theme of America's role in the world throughout the presidential campaign of 1912, he remarked in Detroit: "I believe that light to shine out of the heavens that God himself has created. I believe in human liberty as I believe in the wine of life. . . . America has promised herself and promised the world this great heritage. Shall she break the promise?"[96]

While Wilson lacked experience or specific proposals that he could bring to American international relations, he had a deeply held set of beliefs and a comprehensive philosophy regarding *how* America should relate to the other nations of the world. He knew what his role should be as leader of the nation and had developed a comprehensive *way* of thinking, of balancing antinomies in order to discern the central providential plan. The evidence that he rooted his method of thought in a religious understanding of the world and the progressive millennial views dominant at the time is overwhelming.

March 4, 1913, came to a close. The chief justice had administered the oath of office. Dignitaries had given speeches. The Princeton undergraduates who had escorted the president elect to the capitol were now dispersed. Woodrow Wilson, the twenty-eighth president of the United States, sat that evening in the White House. His election victory had convinced him of the reality of the divine calling that he had sensed throughout his adult life. He would work hard and do his duty to bring God's order to the nation and to the world. The nation was ready. The people had given him God's authority and their own with a constitutional election victory. The world would have to wait until some cataclysmic event signaled that its time had also come.

WW lacked experience in inter'l BUT...

Stacked his high offices
w/ coreligionaus.

2

The Challenge of the Present Age
The Persistence of the International Order

March 1913 was, in a sense, the beginning of a "Presbyterian Camelot." Wanting only the "best men," President Woodrow Wilson chose many associates from the academic world and coreligionists to serve in high offices. A significant part of the new administration shared a basic view of the world as the new president believed the world *should* be. That view would be challenged in their first days in office, however, by the world as it existed, particularly in Mexico and China.

Though personal and policy differences with the president would eventually cause his resignation, Secretary of State William Jennings Bryan was well suited for the administration. Though Bryan was from a less academic and more populist religious tradition than Wilson, both were Presbyterians and shared a similar outlook on the world. Bryan, three times the Democratic Party nominee for president, used his political connections to assure Wilson's nomination at the convention in 1912. Bryan would continue to support the president long after their differences had forced his resignation from the office of secretary of state.

Wilson's views on Bryan went from dislike, to recognition of need, to appreciation when he discovered that the secretary would rarely meddle in sensitive appointments and would leave the president largely free to pursue initiatives in foreign policy.[1] Bryan's willingness to go along with the president was due partly to party loyalty, but fundamentally to the broad areas of agreement that they shared. The secretary of state liked and admired the president. Bryan was chiefly interested in two issues at the beginning of the new administration in 1913: that he would be free to refrain from serving alcohol at official functions, and that he could promote an international peace program.[2] Wilson agreed to both.

Religious leaders in America, like Bryan, found the views Wilson had stated on the campaign trail resonating with their own convictions. The leaders of the Federal Council of Churches, representing the largest group of Protestant churches in America, stirred by the language used during the campaign, wrote to offer congratulations on his victory. They called him a man who had shown by "utterance and action" that "our social order must be fashioned after the Kingdom of God as taught by Jesus Christ."[3] The president believed his administration would work to bring that new social order. In March he wrote to his friend Mary Hulbert: "God give me a clear head, good [counselors] and a pure heart."[4] He now saw the opportunity to fulfill his role as the divine messenger. He was steward of the office, a man with a commission, acting for God and the American people.

Believing politics was "relationships,"[5] but finding the office of the presidency an impersonal duty, Wilson set out to reorder it according to a pattern he was familiar with: the leadership learned from his father.[6] He spoke of his "commissioning" for the task, of the impersonal nature of the administrative apparatus of the presidency, and of his view that he was merely a tool for the job he was called to do. That job required that he be an effective messenger, that he personalize the organization, and that he focus it on the task. He would call the American people to labor in the mission field with him.

This task versus organization language appeared in Wilson's rhetoric from the start of his campaign for the presidency. At Atlantic City in September 1912 he said: "I respect a political party merely as the means of banding men together for a service [after] which, when they have done to the uttermost [sic], they have forgotten parties in a common service."[7] In his Inaugural Address he spoke of his party, which now had a majority in Congress, as meaning "little except when the nation is using [the party] for a large and definite purpose."[8] And shortly after taking office, in Jersey City he said: "I am not a servant of the Democratic party. I am a servant of the people acting through the Democratic party."[9] Calling his political group the "party of the people" was normal partisan rhetoric, but it was rhetoric he believed. He had to believe it. It was the only way his mission could be approved. The organization was only valid if it served the people's purpose, which at this point he equated with God's providence, and was not an end to itself. He continued to operate on the philosophy that "if one sets out to make a by product by itself for itself he spoils the main product."[10] The task he was called to must remain the central focus and *product* of his administration.

His inaugural address spoke to the nation as a Presbyterian minister's sermon might speak to his congregation. The people are a mixture of good and bad, created in the image of God and yet corrupted by sin. The messenger's job is to bring them to repentance from evil and then to call out the best within them. The task of the administration and party was to do the same for the United States. A party not focused on this mission was unfit for the "large and definite purpose" which Wilson envisioned.

> Nowhere else in the world have noble men and women exhibited in more striking forms the beauty and the energy of sympathy and help-fulness . . . in their efforts to rectify wrong, alleviate suffering, and set the weak in the way of strength and hope. . . . But evil has come with the good, and much fine gold has been corroded. With riches has come inexcusable waste. . . . We see the bad with the good, the debased and decadent with the sound and vital. With this vision we approach new affairs. Our duty is to cleanse, to reconsider, to restore, to correct the evil without impairing the good, to purify and humanize every process of our common life without weakening or sentimentalizing it.[11]

The task at hand was the redemption of America. As the appointed messenger of that good news, he called his American congregation to repentance, purification, and reformation. The speech was rife with biblical imagery. There were allusions to the Apostle Paul: "the scales of heedlessness have fallen from our eyes." There were hints from the prophets: "where justice and mercy are reconciled and the judge and the brother are one." He personalized the closing of this speech in language reminiscent of Joshua as Israel entered the promised land. He summoned the people of America, "all honest men, all patriotic, all forward-looking men," to his side. "God helping me, I will not fail them, if they will but counsel and sustain me!"[12] The messenger was ready to lead them to the promised land.

An early domestic issue that foreshadowed the approach he would use in international initiatives was jury reform. Wilson put his office behind this issue in New Jersey, in a speech at Jersey City on May 2nd. It displayed an approach to political power in keeping with the notion of spheres of authority in his covenantal theology. He did not list specific reforms the state should enact. He simply pointed the way and called upon the state government to do the right thing. Believing that his authority in these matters was that of persuasion, he delivered a 'sermon' to the State of New Jersey. His message was a call for justice, an appeal to that which was best in his audience, as his inaugural address said he would do. He finished with a challenge to 'repentance' and commitment to reform.

This pattern of preaching his way to reform by laying out only the broadest of principles would continue throughout his presidency. The actual changes in the jury system were details best left to experts who would work them out along the lines of the principles articulated by the president. Detractors, such as Keynes, saw this avoidance of specifics as words lacking substance. They failed to realize that to Wilson the words were the substance. In language reminiscent of the article "Christ's Army," written in his youth, he stated: "the eventual outcome of the day of battle is not in doubt. There is a God in the heavens, and all is well. And I am not going to be impatient."[13] The United States had become the parish of political pastor Woodrow Wilson.

The president initially viewed himself as a sort of instructor in chief, but hoped to become more than that.[14] He hoped, if possible, to write his political autobiography on the politics of the world as well. For the moment he believed the great powers were beyond instruction. Latin America and Asia (minus Japan), however, were ripe for American tutelage. In his mind Japan had become a difficult student, a competitor to U.S. interests in Asia, a colonial power on a similar level to the Europeans.

The vast and ancient land of China, on the other hand, was a different situation. It was a land of great missionary exploits. It held great potential as a laboratory for democracy. Many American business interests also saw a great opportunity in China with its massive population. The two visions, business and missionary democracy, were in competition. The administration of President William Howard Taft had embraced the idea of civilizing China through expanding trade, the idea embodied in "dollar diplomacy." Wilson despised this approach. As historian Michael Hunt has pointed out: "Wilson's own clear conception of the obligation of the United States [was] to promote the modern trinity—democracy, the rule of law, and Christianity."[15] He would be an evangelist, a missionary, for the export of Christian democracy. The United States would offer the gospel of democracy to the world.

The argument that Wilson wanted to project this missionary image of the United States to the world is supported by his attempt to appoint John R. Mott ambassador to China. Mott was a noted missionary. He had devoted his life to mission work. After finishing a degree in history at Cornell, Mott became national secretary for the YMCA in the United States and Canada, chairman of the executive committee of the Student Volunteer Movement for Foreign Missions, presiding officer of the World Missionary Conference and chairman of the International Missionary Council. He had organized the World's Student Christian Federation, and at the time Wilson was looking to fill the post in Beijing, Mott was also general-secretary of the International Committee of the YMCA. He was a missionary's missionary.

The president's first choice for China had been Dr. Charles Eliot, president of Harvard. When Eliot declined for health reasons Wilson quickly, and with little apparent regret, turned to Mott. Mott represented Wilson's vision of America's mission to the world. The clear lines between good and evil that missionaries represented appealed to the president. He believed America's role in the world was compatible with, and could work in parallel with, Christian evangelism. He united the goals of missionaries with the aims of the United States government.

As a result, the president became personally invested in Mott's nomination. The lengths to which Wilson went to recruit Mott and the language he used in this attempt are telling. Two weeks before the inaugural Wilson wrote Bryan regarding China and Mott: "The Christian influence, direct or indirect, is very prominently at the front and I need not say, ought to be kept there."[16] He asserted that Mott possessed the qualities of a statesman and the "confidence of those throughout the Christian world." He was the kind of "best" Wilson was looking for in a subordinate, a true Christian statesman. When his nominee turned down the appointment, rather than accepting the answer as he had done with Eliot, the president began to lobby friends to pressure Mott to accept.[17] In the following weeks Wilson enlisted any friend of Mott's he could find to join him in this effort. He refused to accept Mott's rejection of the post twice, stating that the "interests of China and the Christian world are so intimately involved."[18] He even went to the extraordinary step of suggesting that Mott keep his mission post while acting as ambassador. The president would grant him leave of absence to do missionary work as necessary. "I am eager to unite what you represent with what this government means to try to represent."[19] Mott was finally able to turn the China post down on April 1st.[20]

The biggest area of concern in U.S. foreign policy before the outbreak of war in Europe, however, was Latin America. It became the first test of the new administration's missionary foreign policy. In February 1913, a revolution in Mexico led by Victoriano Huerta overthrew the government of President Francisco Madero. Huerta had Madero jailed, then arranged his assassination. Mexico split into warring factions. The North was occupied by the forces of occasional allies, Venustiano Carranza and Francisco "Pancho" Villa. The south was a mountainous region partly controlled by Emiliano Zapata. Huerta controlled the center of the country, including the capital. This unrest in Mexico created concern in the United States, its direct neighbor to the north, and threatened American investments. The Mexican crisis was fully developed by the time Wilson took office, so he had to focus his immediate attention on the region.

On March 12, 1913, the White House released a general statement on U.S. relations with Latin America. The Cabinet devoted an entire day to its preparation.[21] The importance that both Wilson and Bryan put on the document itself showed the degree to which they saw word as action. The time spent by the entire Cabinet discussing this single short statement, along with the great hope held that it alone would "stop those who foment troubles," was revealing.[22]

To Wilson and Bryan, words were acts. Wilson was the divinely appointed messenger, now addressing an international as well as a national congregation. His view concerning the power of the spoken message was outlined in a speech he had given on December 17, 1912. Nothing was permanent, he remarked, "except the thoughts which you spoke to your neighbors."[23] Thoughts embodied in words were substance. They held ideas which would continue to create a reality when the material body was gone. His December 17 speech, the Latin American statement, and the care with which it was prepared, demonstrated how the president translated this high view of language into political practice.

The Latin American statement stressed the need for orderly constitutional processes: government based on the consent of the governed. It proclaimed that the United States had no interest in "Central and South America except the lasting interests of the peoples of the two continents."[24] The words were pleasant and diplomatic enough, but they did not reflect the reality of U.S. relations with Latin America. The expressed views ran contrary to the interests of American businesses, which were already in direct relationships with the very forces denounced in the statement as using "arbitrary or irregular force" in order to "seize the power of government to advance their own personal interests or ambition."[25] The president did not propose any specific action to end these relationships or to moderate American business practices in Latin America. Nevertheless, he did not believe his speech was empty rhetoric. Words had the power to create reality by harnessing the imagination of men. He coupled that imaginative power to faith.[26] The conflict between word and reality was only "apparent" and temporary. These apparent contradictions would work in harmony to cause the intended outcome if time were allowed for the words to produce their fruit.

The situation in Mexico was a demonstration of how Wilson's application of antinomy to foreign policy decision making worked. The president began by working through the contradiction in his mind. Once he had reconciled the antinomies and determined the right course, he acted. He developed his thinking about intervention in foreign countries in a manner consistent with the way he

balanced historical contradictions the country had already faced in international politics. He was critical of American action in the 1846 Mexican War. In *A History of the American People*, he called it "inexcusable aggression."[27] He subsequently rejected Taft's formulation of "dollar diplomacy" as a violation of the national sovereignty of weaker nations. His treatment of the 1898 war with Spain, however, expressed a different point of view. Despite calling it a war of *impulse* and acknowledging the sensational, exaggerated newspaper accounts and the personal ambition and desire to aggrandize American power that motivated some participants, he also felt the war was justified by the intransigence and evil of the Spanish government. Spain forced American action by sinking the battleship *Maine*. The war was also just because it was fought to liberate the oppressed and suffering subjects of Spain in Cuba. This made the war an *unselfish thing*. Doing the right, unselfish thing allowed providence to bless America with unintended but good consequences. The *selfless* sacrifice of the soldiers in the Spanish-American War had created an environment in which healing had come to the sectional divisions left following the Civil War. This logic followed Wilson's Presbyterian view of human nature as flawed by sin yet still able to act righteously when called to serve a higher purpose.[28] A righteous cause would have unintended righteous, and providential, consequences. When antinomy made logic unclear, the right course of action was to determine the righteous cause. Once the right thing to do was settled, a righteous leader simply did his duty. Though at first it might appear complicated and he could only "see through a glass darkly," if he stayed the course all would eventually become clear.[29]

Wilson applied this balance of principles to the muddy world of Mexican politics. It was not an easy balance to maintain. To begin with, there was question about who was the "legitimate" representative of the people in Mexico. The president quickly determined that it could never be Huerta and refused to grant recognition to that regime. The means by which he had gained power disqualified him. The northen forces who opposed Huerta called themselves "Constitutionalists," a name that immediately appealed to Wilson.[30] Reality was quite different from the name, however, and American citizens and property fared better in the areas controlled by Federal forces than they did in the areas held by the Constitutionalists. It was also clear to American observers that the Constitutionalists were not united. Villa and Carranza were rivals bound only by the thin cord of opposition to Huerta. They neither liked nor trusted each other. There was no guarantee that they would hold together, much less win the contest. The forces with Zapata in the south, though not powerful enough to overcome Huerta, added pressure and complication to the precarious Constitutionalist alliance. Wilson's view of Mexico in his mind was much clearer than the situation in Mexico actually was.[31]

The information reaching the president regarding Mexico was confusing and spotty, but he paid more attention to it than he would during later international challenges when forced by health and the convergence of multiple crises to make snap judgments on superficial information. He removed the U.S. ambassador to Mexico, Henry Lane Wilson, early in the crisis, in part as a protest to Huerta and in part because of his dubious political loyalties to the administration.[32] The ambassador, a Taft appointee, had little motivation to support the policies of the new Democratic administration. The chargé d'affaires in Mexico City, Nelson O'Shaughnessy, tried his best to represent the U.S. In hope of furthering U.S. interests he became close to Huerta, who in turn called him "son." While O'Shaughnessy liked Huerta and viewed his own president's instructions as "asinine," he carried those instructions out scrupulously and loyally.[33] He also sent good information to Washington. This did not reduce the president's skepticism toward the reports he received. In part because the information did not conform to his already conceived view of the Mexican situation and, in part, because he was not generally trustful of the information he received from his State Department, the president relied more upon his private sources than O'Shaughnessy.

In keeping with his pattern of *personalizing* the mission, the president commissioned friends to go to Mexico on his behalf. He first asked a journalist, William Hale, to go so that he might get reports "unofficially and through the eyes of an independent observer."[34] Hale spoke no Spanish and had to rely on translators to gather his information. This was the type of "unbiased" information Wilson preferred. His own government was an organization that might or might not be advancing the higher purpose for which it was intended. He wanted a personal messenger. He also wanted someone who knew as little as possible about Mexico, to see the situation with fresh eyes. It was a common joke in Washington at the time that "among the people who came to Washington eager to lay their knowledge of Mexican conditions before him that the only way to get to him was to tell Tumulty that you had never been in Mexico."[35]

Another set of eyes that the president sent to observe the situation in Mexico was John Lind. A former governor of Minnesota, anxious to involve himself in the mission of "redeeming" the country, Lind saw the world much as Wilson did.[36] Speaking no Spanish and with a strong anti-Catholic bias, Lind went to Mexico in August 1913 and began to send back regular reports to the president. Along with those of Lind, Hale, and O'Shaughnessy, numerous reports from other sources, official and unofficial, came back to Washington. Upon this mountain of information Wilson stamped his idea of divine order. He accepted that which strengthened his preconceived view, but rejected or reinterpreted that which contradicted it.

There are direct parallels to Wilson's views on Mexico as expressed in 1913 and the views that he espoused in his 1879 article, "Self Government in France."[37] He saw in the Mexicans the same tendency toward centralized government, a society that stumbled between despotism and disorder, and a people incapable of moderate constitutional action. He saw large landowning classes, a centralized Roman Catholic church and a dissident underclass that vacillated between revolution and passivity in the face of despotism.[38] Nevertheless, Mexico had one great difference. Unlike France, it was in the New World. Its population was made up largely of an uneducated, darker skinned people whom the United States could instruct. Wilson told Sir William Tyrrell, the personal secretary to Foreign Secretary Sir Edward Grey who was acting on behalf of the British Government in Washington during the illness of Ambassador Sir Cecil Spring Rice, that he had decided to "teach these countries a lesson by insisting on the removal of Huerta."[39] Until the Mexican people produced their own "divine messenger," the American president would fill their pulpit as interim minister.

Wilson had grown up with a specific Christian teaching regarding what actions were righteous and what actions were evil. Righteous action was that which was motivated by obedience to God's law, by love for God and one's fellow man, by service not selfishness. An unrighteous act was one motivated by some self-gratifying purpose. Selfless action was a key to the Calvinist conception of just war. The evils of war and the preferability of peace had been reinforced by Wilson's childhood experience in the South. Growing up during the Civil War and Reconstruction and seeing firsthand the devastation that war had on human life had marked his attitudes and blunted his desire to use military force. Still, war was not always the wrong course of action. Though evil, it might still be a necessary evil. Wilson was not a pacifist, he simply knew the evils of war.[40]

It was the motivation for war that determined whether the participant was acting according to God's will or not. This inner motivation allowed him to honor the soldiers who fought in war even if he felt that the motives for the war itself were mixed. Soldiers could be pure in their motivation in that they were serving the higher good of their country. They did their duty and put their lives on the line. If there was someone to blame, or if the war was selfish and unjust, that charge must be laid against their leaders. A just war was not to be conducted against people but against bad systems. It was organizations, governments, or systems that were evil and must be struggled against. Taking a line of logic directly from Paul's letter to the Ephesians, the very passage he used in his article, "Christ's Army," he said: "I am not interested in fighting persons, but I am interested in fighting things. I am interested in fighting bad tendencies, bad systems, things that lower all the levels of our political and economic morality."[41]

Wilson had balanced the issues of war and peace his whole life. In his address on the Bible in Denver, shortly before he ran for president, Governor Wilson spoke in the same terms he had always used concerning the war for righteousness.

> No man can sit down and withhold his hands from warfare against wrong and get peace out of his acquiescence. The most solid and satisfying peace is that which comes from this constant spiritual warfare, and there originate times in the history of nations when they must take up the crude instruments of bloodshed in order to vindicate spiritual conceptions. For liberty is a spiritual conception, and when men take up arms to set other men free, there is something sacred and holy in

the warfare. I will not cry "Peace" so long as there is sin and wrong in the world.[42]

The United States might be forced to use its military as a response to the evil in Mexico.[43] That use, if it came from an unselfish motivation and had an unselfish goal, would be just.

Despite his view that war was not fought against the people but against bad systems that prevented people from living free, Wilson did not have a developed sense of institutional evil such as the youthful Reinhold Niebuhr was developing as he watched world events unfold. Wilson's ideas about the righteousness of the United States with respect to the use of force in Mexico originated from his beliefs about individual morality which he transferred to this international situation. In the antinomy between the individual and government, the government, as a group of individuals and as an organization, was subordinate to its service and mission to people. His illustrations as to why the nation might have to go to war show this individual morality written upon his views of national and systemic morality. Later, in May 1916, he would remark on this idea to the National Press Club: "If I cannot retain my moral influence over a man except by occasionally knocking him down, . . . then for the sake of his soul I have got to occasionally knock him down."[44] Though he spoke of American military force being used to retain "moral influence" over another country, his illustration compared that use with individual action. To Wilson, the problems in Mexico were just personal human problems writ large. This also had the effect of simplifying complex problems into manageable concepts.

An irony produced by the tensions of Wilson's approach was that despite his rhetorical commitment to fight systems rather than people, he personalized conflict in his own mind, focusing on national leaders whom he considered evil. The individual personalities and motives of the officials of other governments often became central as he negotiated international crises. If they were evil, or opposed the United States, these leaders were also inevitably opposed to the will of their own people. This approach made it difficult to see how his policies were opposing systems when he made the opposition so personal. The first item of information Wilson wanted from House at the outbreak of war in Europe concerned the personalities of the European heads of state.[45] The information that Wilson most wanted from Hale, his "independent observer" in Mexico, was an assessment of the personalities of the Mexican leaders.[46] It was how he united the concurrent principles of his covenant theology, divine mission, redemptive purpose and American power with his commission as president. He brought all the strands of purpose and organization together in himself. Privately he told House that he believed the executive was the institutional leader of the collective desires of the people. As such, opposition to him was opposition to the desires of the people. International conflicts boiled down to a contest between two leaders, embodying two systems, one good, the other evil.[47]

At a Jackson Day speech in 1915, Wilson went further. He said that while Jackson thought that every man who disagreed with him was an enemy of the country, he himself had, "never gone quite that far in my thoughts, but I have ventured to think that they didn't know what they were talking about. . . ."[48] Personal leadership transcended the government and individualized the "desires of the people." Since "providence ordered the affairs of men," and since those men had chosen him and embodied their will in him, it could be deduced that he was the delegated voice of God, a modern Moses by both democratic and divine election.[49]

Business interests were lower on the president's list of priorities than other, less tangible, interests. It would be inaccurate to describe Wilson as "anti-business." It would be equally difficult to describe him as "pro-business" in his international relations policy. Other than a commitment to helping the "little guy" of small business, the president could best be described as benignly neutral toward large international business interests.[50] Many business leaders in the U.S. pressured the president to act on their behalf in Mexico. He would not do so unless they could convince him of a *righteous* reason. He was prompted by the thought of *saving* the oppressed people of Mexico, but it was obvious to most observers at the time that neither Wilson nor Bryan paid much attention to American business interests in Mexico. The president even refused to provide extra transport, other than the naval vessels already there, to evacuate American citizens, most of whom were connected to U.S. businesses in Mexico.[51]

Wilson made the position he would take on American business in Mexico clear when he publicly rejected "dollar diplomacy" in a speech on March 18, 1913. He specifically rejected a set of loan initiatives proposed by the Taft administration.[52] The main focus of those initiatives was American loans to China, but they had included Latin America as well.[53] Wilson's concern was that these loans infringed upon the sovereignty of the nations to whom the loans went. They violated the orderly covenantal process. In another speech the previous December he argued that: "the service of humanity is the best business of mankind, and that the business of mankind must be set forward by the governments which mankind sets up, in order that justice may be done and mercy not forgotten."[54] Banks did not have the same covenantal task as governments.[55] Business interests must not dominate the sovereignty of a country. Business had not been given that task. Divine order in Mexico required a government freely chosen by the people. Banks were not ordained by God to make policy themselves. Returning his rhetoric to the need for that mysterious accountability of the heart to the divine order which superceded organization and human law, Wilson added: "There must be heart in government; there must be a heart in the policies of government. And men must look to it that they do unto others as they would have others do unto them."[56] Banks would not look out for the people's interest in Mexico. He applied the task versus organization antinomy to dollar diplomacy. The organizational task of banks was to make money. The organizational task of his administration was to bring democracy and good government to the people of Mexico. Money interests, left unchecked, would resist that mission.

On October 27, 1913 Wilson spelled out his alternative to dollar diplomacy in a speech to the Southern Commercial Congress in Mobile, Alabama. He talked of the "spiritual" nature of the relationship between the nations in the Americas.[57] The larger powers had victimized these nations. They had not done unto them as they would have desired to be done unto. None of the great powers would allow "concessions" to another country within their own borders. Yet they routinely required them of the smaller countries in Latin America.[58] Wilson sketched out his plan: "The United States will never again seek one additional foot of territory by conquest."[59] America conveyed an idea of individual opportunity and liberty. While this would take work and time, America would lead the world to new heights of justice. It was the American destiny. He closed the speech with the biblical imagery of climbing the mountain of the Lord. ". . . slowly ascending the tedious climb that leads to the final uplands, we shall get our ultimate view of the duties of mankind. . . . presently—it may be in a generation or two—[we shall] come out on those great heights where shines, unobstructed, the light of the justice of God."[60] The imagery of Moses climbing the mountain to view the promised land, or the psalmist speaking of the righteous ascending the mountain of the Lord, is unmistakable. Wilson saw his Latin American policy as a righteous endeavor. Force would only be used as a tool in the service of righteousness.

The president's new program was tested at the port of Veracruz. Historian Robert Quirk has written that, in light of the benevolent idealism which Wilson believed his policies in Latin America represented, it is ironic that Mexican historians express greater disdain for the intervention at Veracruz than to the outright land grab of the Mexican War of 1846.[61] By personalizing the foreign policy of the United States to the degree that he did, by cloaking it with the language of a clearly defined morality and righteousness, Wilson created a greater hatred of his policies than he might have had he openly pursued a traditional great power strategy. He spoke of his policies with language appropriate to a coming peaceful millennial age while using the common tools of the present age: power and military force. To those not able to peer into the antinomy of his heart, Wilson looked like a moralistic, self-righteous hypocrite. On his part, however, elevating the issues to the level of moral principle left no room to compromise and heightened the stakes.

The stakes were already high. In the days leading up to the Mobile speech Wilson drafted a *Circular Note to the Powers*, in which he said that the United States would not recognize the Huerta government. That government "was conceived in absolutism fastened upon the country by methods abhorrent to the conscience of the world."[62] Just as the U.S. had been willing to intervene to liberate Cuba from foreign political power, it would now be willing to keep Mexico free from foreign financial power. He was willing to use the Monroe Doctrine as justification for preventing foreign commercial interests from exploiting the internal affairs of Mexico.

The rhetoric from the president indicated that he was committed to both nonintervention and the forces of constitutional democracy in Mexico. The reality was not nearly so clear. Despite the rebels' rejection of what Wilson said the United States was supporting, he directed Bryan to affirm strong U.S. support for them as early as December 1913.[63] Rationalizing that he had picked the side that supported the spirit of democracy, if not yet its form, and believing he was acting in his role of God's chosen agent, he tailored his policy decisions to negotiate the antinomy between what his principles espoused and the reality in Mexico. The will of God (the right thing) would ultimately happen so long as his acts were righteous. He was confident that his conscience was qualified to determine what those righteous acts were. By February 1914 the U.S. was openly supporting the Constitutionalist forces. This decision was made despite their use of unconstitutional means to gain power. By November it had become clear to Wilson's representatives that the Constitutionalists had priorities other than democracy. They would not allow democratic processes until they had achieved military success and broken the power of the church, wealthy landowners, and Huerta's military.[64] This mattered little to the president, who had made up his mind that the Constitutionalist cause was righteous.

Wilson explained his decision to throw American influence behind these forces who were using less than constitutional means to gain power to Spring Rice. The United States had a "moral duty" toward a weaker state on the American continent.[65] That duty took precedence over the organization of a constitutional government in Mexico. The letter of the law, the legalist approach to constitutional government, could not stand in the way of the task of creating a mature democracy in Mexico. A radical revolution was needed in Mexico to clear the way for constitutional change. It was too early to force organizational, constitutional, and legal reform before order was brought to the country and the people were able to express their will, their spirit in constitutional leaders. The spirit always preceded the law. No one had yet emerged as the clear leader of Mexico, able to embody the spirit of the Mexican people. To Wilson, the hindrances to this emerging democracy were economic more than political. Until the powerful money interests were broken, true constitutional government could not emerge. Any government that emerged prior to that, being dominated by these monied interests, might actually hinder democracy in Mexico.[66] The task was of greater importance than the legal mechanics of democracy. True democracy would spring up naturally, under U.S. tutelage, once the right leaders who embodied the will of the people had emerged.

For the present there was nothing the United States could do. Spring Rice quoted the president saying the Mexican people must "find their own salvation." In fact Wilson most likely said "They must work out their own salvation," a biblical quotation he would have been familiar with, indicating that they needed to do the hard work of bringing their own society into order.[67] He made it clear that he had no interest in helping the wealthy retain their position, but he did want to work to help the poor of Mexican society, those who could not help themselves. For them, and for their instruction, he was willing to find a way to bring about salvation, to create conditions in which the poor could save themselves. Wilson continued to demonstrate an unwavering faith in providence in his approach to Mexico. Neither he nor Bryan had a clear idea of how to handle the chaos that would follow the collapse of the Huerta government, but they had no particular worries about it either. The fall of Huerta was a moral duty, and as such the situation would right itself if America did the right thing. Wilson continued to base United States policy on the mystery of providence. Obey God, work hard, and all would work out in the end.

With all else in place, Wilson needed to wait until the right time, a providential moment, to act in Mexico. All other elements were present for righteous action: an oppressed people, an aggressive evil power, a *selfless* motive to intervene. The only thing left was an incident of aggression by the evil power that would allow America to defend the righteous. The point for domestic reform had come to America with Wilson's election. The time to act in Mexico needed that moment as well. The necessary impetus turned out to be the Tampico incident. Wilson referred to this as the "psychological moment."[68] It provided him with the necessary rationalization for action.

Tampico was a comparatively minor incident between American sailors and Federal forces loyal to the Huerta government. Its only significance was that it gave Wilson justification for his determined righteous action in Mexico. The incident demonstrated his preferred methodology for handling complicated foreign policy matters. It was a pattern that would be repeated throughout his presidency. On April 9, 1914, a small squad of U.S. sailors in a whaleboat entered the mouth of the river in the port of Tampico, a point contested by the opposing sides in the Mexican conflict. The American forces had not notified the Federal commander of their intentions to land at that point. Federal troops arrested the crew when they discovered the Americans loading gasoline into their boat from a dock near the battle line. The Mexican soldiers took their prisoners to police headquarters, where the Mexican commander promptly released them with an apology to the American commander, Admiral Henry Mayo.

Mayo, however, demanded more than the apology given. He demanded a further, formal, written apology, with a guarantee that the officer responsible would be punished followed by a twenty-one gun salute to the American flag. This escalated a minor incident into the beginnings of a major crisis. Since the United States had refused to recognize the Huerta government, this added demand constituted an unbearable humiliation.

The admiral's dispatch, with sparse and misleading information about the incident, arrived in Washington on April 10th. Bryan forwarded it to Wilson with the comment: "I do not see that Mayo could have done otherwise."[69] The president, on vacation and deeply concerned about his ailing wife, fired back a message to Bryan further escalating the incident. He demanded that O'Shaughnessy take up the matter of Mayo's demands with Huerta in Mexico City and press it with the utmost earnestness, "representing to them its extreme seriousness." He had already decided that this was the moment to engage the righteous fight. The president directed that Secretary of the Navy Josephus Daniels "impress upon his officers the absolute necessity of being entirely in the right," and added as an afterthought that State Department Counselor Robert Lansing "can of course supply you with precedents."[70]

The president had made up his mind without making any effort to confirm Mayo's report, much less to confirm whether the admiral's action was appropriate under international law. The process of decision-making which he demonstrated in this incident set a pattern for future issues.[71] Lansing's expertise in international law was to serve the president by finding the right precedent to support the course Wilson had already determined to take. International law served a righteous purpose, it did not determine if the purpose was righteous. Lansing did not disappoint the president, though it took him four days of searching and he had to go back sixty years to find a legal precedent which would justify unilateral American action. Charles Thompson, an observer during this period, commented that "Wilson never distrusted himself about anything, being more positive that he was invariably right than any man I ever saw."[72] During this period, House recounted how the president privately asserted that he always sought others' advice. While managing to keep a straight face in front of the president he noted that evening in his journal that he had nearly laughed out loud.[73]

Wilson limited his reading of potential evidence on foreign policy issues to a minimum, partly as a result of ill health and partly to keep his mind from the clutter of too much detail.[74] On Mexico he had made up his mind. After reading Mayo's report he saw no reason to belabor or reconsider the decision. He needed to act. Mexico must be brought into righteous order. Lansing's discovery of a precedent lent a helpful air of international legality. Wilson already considered the action legal, however, because it was in accordance with his own vision of a higher law, whether or not it was supported by treaties or jurists. Within hours of Lansing's fortuitous discovery, the Atlantic fleet was ordered to Mexico to reinforce the ships already outside Tampico and Veracruz. A flurry of urgent diplomatic communication followed. Washington was never quite sure of what was happening as each perceived crisis gave way to the next. This was not, however, of immediate concern to the president. The specific details of each day's crisis were of little relevance to Wilson in light of the larger task of bringing order to Mexico.

Meanwhile, in Mexico City, O'Shaugnessy was largely kept in the dark. Wilson's practice of using personal emissaries while bypassing his own official representatives created confusion for U.S. diplomats and foreign governments. This confusion increased in Mexico as the chargé continued to presume he was still speaking for the United States. O'Shaughnessy worked faithfully to represent his government's interests, though often without any clear knowledge as to what its intentions were or how it defined those interests. In fact, he only discovered that there had been an incident at Tampico when representatives of the Mexican government approached him to get the U.S. response. Communication through the diplomatic corps was on autopilot. The president was not using, or even informing, his official diplomats.[75]

On April 14, Wilson issued a press release regarding the situation in Mexico. It was riddled with inaccuracies that various dispatches had conveyed to Washington.[76] O'Shaughnessy, trying to do his job, used his friendship with Huerta to try to persuade the Mexican leader to accommodate American demands. Wilson, who could tolerate no compromise with evil, viewed the closeness of O'Shaughnessy with Huerta as a prime example of what was wrong with the diplomatic corps. In the end, his hard work to resolve the Mexican crisis doomed the young diplomat's career.[77]

The American hard line in Tampico created a political impasse for Huerta. The weakened Mexican federal government could not afford to appear to capitulate to humiliating American demands. Huerta was not able to respond to Wilson's call to repentance. He had read the mood of his citizens correctly and knew that an American invasion would do more to help him in their eyes than it would to hurt him. Huerta chose to defy the president, refusing to sacrifice his honor or that of Mexico over such a minor incident.

Diplomatic communications went back and forth between the two determined national leaders. Bryan, for whom peace was the ultimate goal, went from elation to despair and back again with each succeeding report. Wilson, with his larger goal of world order in mind, remained clear and steadfast in his decision to act, displaying little apparent emotional fluctuation. He had determined what action the United States should take. He would let the situation play itself out to its providential end. The detailed information coming into Washington seemed incidental to his decision. He was certain that the policy of the U.S. was right and would be welcomed by the Mexican people.

He was, after all, acting as their savior. House wrote in his journal that the president told him privately: "When a man's house is on fire he should be glad if his neighbors help him out."[78]

The stalemate came to an end at two o'clock on the morning of April 21. The State Department learned that a German vessel was approaching Veracruz with an arms shipment for the Huerta government. Convincing a reluctant White House staff to awaken the president, Bryan was able to deliver the news. With no hesitation, the president ordered troops ashore to seize the customs house at Veracruz. He then returned to bed. Congressional approval for the military action had not yet been given, but the president lost no sleep over legal unpleasantness. The pieces were now in place for righteous action. Though the seizure of Veracruz seemed to some a direct contradiction of his earlier statement in Mobile, "the United States will never again seek one additional foot of territory by conquest," there was no contradiction in Wilson's mind. His motive was pure and unselfish. The United States was not conquering Veracruz, it was protecting the interests of the Mexican people, which were threatened by their own government.[79] The U.S. was still a neutral party. While others worried about consequences, Wilson continued to believe that if he did his duty, obeyed God, and worked hard, all would work out right in the end. He was convinced that his actions would bring divine order to the chaos.

In Mexico as elsewhere the president believed the outcome, now in the hands of providence, would work out for a better world. All the evidence thus far in his career seemed to prove that this was the path to success. His apparent setbacks, such as the losing battle with the Princeton board of trustees, had resulted through the mystery of providence in his rise to the presidency of the most powerful nation in the world. Sticking to his principles would continue to work, so he saw no incentive to change his methods.

American sailors and marines landed in Veracruz. They were greeted with bullets rather than open arms. The local population joined the Federal soldiers in armed resistance. At least two hundred Mexicans were killed and many more wounded. Nineteen American soldiers and sailors were killed and forty-seven wounded. Worse for Wilson's hopes of tutoring the Mexicans in good government, after

Veracruz was captured, few municipal officials were willing to work for the United States. They cited their sense of patriotism as well as fear of reprisal from Mexican authorities when the territory was returned to Mexico. The U.S. military was forced to occupy the entire city and establish martial law. Veracruz proved a diplomatic disaster for the United States. The warring factions in Mexico united in anger at the invasion of their sovereign territory. Rather than being treated as a helpful neighbor by the owner of a burning house as Wilson had portrayed the action to House, the Americans were looked upon as burglars breaking into the house while the owners were involved in a domestic dispute. Huerta expelled the hapless O'Shaughnessy following the seizure. Wilson never employed the young diplomat again in any position of note in U.S. diplomatic service. The administration's policy met severe opposition in the Senate. Senator Henry Cabot Lodge of Massachusetts complained: "Any man who did not think the facts ought to be made to suit his will would have known that the people of Veracruz would fight."[80]

As the controversy raged in Washington and elsewhere in Latin America, U.S. troops set about organizing a military government to administer Veracruz. Argentina, Brazil, and Chile (whose representatives would become the ABC commission) offered to meet in a neutral country to mediate the conflict. The United States accepted the mediation, but on grounds that doomed it to failure. Wilson, convinced that the United States was acting in the best interests of Mexico, and as such was neutral, attempted to bring the negotiations to the United States. Huerta refused to consider the United States neutral and the talks were moved to Niagara Falls, Canada, a few hundred feet from the American border. The president insisted that the United States would participate only as a neutral observer. He persisted in the idea that the U.S. was benign in the conflict, interested only in obtaining an end to the Huerta regime for the good of the Mexican people. Carranza refused to send any delegates at all, rejecting negotiation with Huerta over elections or the U.S. over an illegal invasion of his country. Huerta thought that the purpose of the negotiations was to come to an agreement with the U.S. over the removal of its troops from Mexico, a view shared by the ABC commissioners. Eventually realizing that the "discussions" were utterly pointless, the commissioners gave up and went home on July 2nd.[81]

Wilson never altered his principles or changed his view of the international situation to conform to these developments. He still saw no place for compromise. As he had written in "Christ's Army" so many years earlier, "there is no middle course, no neutrality. Each one must enlist either with the followers of Christ or those of Satan."[82] Though the truth may be an intellectual antinomy, clear to God but not to man, it was still truth and any resistance to its "principle" was opposition, not just to the idea of truth, but to Christ himself. Wilson was determined to instruct Mexico in the right way to govern itself. He explained his policy to Tyrrell: "I am going to teach the South American Republics to elect good men."[83]

Resisting pressure from both those who wanted to order the military to push on to Mexico City and end the crisis by force and those who wanted to remove the troops in order to seek a diplomatic solution, the president hovered between peace and war. He instructed the military to put Veracruz in order. They set about the task with zeal. The market was cleaned up, a police force was organized, the courts put in order, streets were cleaned and sanitary measures imposed. Veracruz was an apparent model of Wilson's view of an ordered world. In a manner that would have both honored and satirized Calvin's theocratic Geneva, Veracruz became, as a historian of the affair has written, "the cleanest, most efficient, most honest and just" despotism in Mexico.[84]

On July 15, Huerta, his forces routed by the advancing Constitutionalist armies, resigned and went into exile. Wilson was overjoyed. This joy was quickly dampened by Carranza's response to his victory. Continued revolution, not free elections, would be the policy of the new government. He promised to punish those who had helped the Americans at Veracruz. Those who had cooperated with Wilson's tutoring in democracy were to be penalized by their own new government, which Wilson had enabled to come to power. The result was another diplomatic deadlock over principle. Eventually, necessity dictated that Carranza concede, at least verbally, to get U.S. forces to leave Veracruz. Wilson accepted Carranza's word.

After regaining Veracruz, Carranza's forces punished those who had collaborated with the Americans, despite his promise to the president. Wilson would never again trust a Mexican leader; words were, after all, real to Wilson. A few months after the American marines had left Veracruz there was little evidence they had ever been there.

The Veracruz intervention could have become a lesson to the administration on the limits of power. It did not, however, because Wilson could not recognize the need for such a lesson. Instead he repeated the scenario at Veracruz in varying forms throughout his terms in office. The same pattern is evident in the motivation and outcome of the interventions in Santo Domingo, Haiti, Nicaragua, Russia, and the European War. It was deeply rooted in Wilson's idea of principle and his view of the world as he believed it should be. To the end, he held the conviction that the United States, if it acted righteously, would always come out on top. Though the temporary situation might look as if it was not turning out well, it would do so in the end. Any apparent failure in Mexico was only apparent. The working out of God's will over time would justify American action.

Wilson remained convinced that America, by acting on God's behalf, was above the venal politics of "this present age." Thus it could remain neutral even as it used its military and economic power to produce the righteous outcome. American troops could invade and occupy Mexican territory, but America was not an occupier. The U.S. could violate all the accepted standards of neutrality as spelled out by international law and still be neutral by a higher law. The United States was on God's side, not that of any political entity.

Before the Mexican situation was resolved, other events had distracted the president. In August 1914 his wife Ellen died. That same week the armies of Europe launched a suicidal war. Mexico, which would occupy a place of interest in U.S. foreign policy throughout the rest of the Wilson administration and briefly, thanks to the Zimmermann telegram, inject itself into U.S.–German relations, was largely buried in importance by an avalanche of other personal and international concerns.

3

Keeping to the Principles in Peace and War

On June 28, 1914, in Sarajevo in the Austro-Hungarian province of Bosnia, the Austrian Archduke Franz Ferdinand and his wife were assassinated by a Serbian student, thereby setting in motion the chain of events that would plunge Europe into war. The European alliance system broke down, setting in motion a number of diplomatic blunders. The resulting failures culminated with the great powers going to war. The president of the United States and his administration tried to find ways to use the good offices of the United States to mediate the peace.[1] These efforts were barely noticed in Europe and, after the assassination of the Archduke, failed to prevent the outbreak of hostilities in August 1914.

That August was also marked by a personal crisis that competed for the president's attention with the chaos and death into which Europe was plunging itself. Ellen, his wife, solace, and confidante died from the complications of Bright's disease five weeks after their twenty-ninth wedding anniversary. This tragedy created an intensive inner conflict for the president. His Calvinist world view, combined with his belief that divinely directed history was an orderly process, generated for him a vision of the world toward which he believed that both he and history were progressing. Wilson's inner providential picture of how things should be included the presence of Ellen. He needed a woman's love and devotion. Ellen played her part as companion and advisor masterfully. She had smoothed over conflict and aided in the president's professional and political successes.[2] He relied on her for emotional security. As she grew increasingly ill during the

spring of 1914, he remained optimistic in the face of overwhelming evidence that she was dying. As late as July 28 Wilson continued to insist that there was nothing physically wrong with his wife.
Though the people around the president had initially kept much of
the bad news away from him at the behest of the president's physi-
cian, Admiral Cary Grayson, his optimism continued even after they
had informed him that Ellen's condition was terminal.[3] He sat by her
bedside as he worked, writing with one hand while holding hers in
the other. By August 2, four days before her death, her health and the
situation in Europe competed equally for his attention.[4] On August
6, the day she died, against overwhelming evidence and long after any
reasonable hope for recovery had vanished, he wrote his brother that
there was still hope and that he would let him know if there was any
turn in her condition either way.[5] The turn had come months before.
When House received the word that Ellen had died it stunned him.
None of the president's letters to him had suggested the seriousness of
her condition.[6]

Ellen's death devastated Wilson. It seemed to be a contradiction
to providence. It was inconceivable that God's plan did not include
Ellen by his side. He simply had not considered life without Ellen a
possibility. The shock turned his emotional world upside down. "God
has stricken me almost beyond what I can bear," he wrote to his friend
Mary Hulbert.[7] He felt that nothing was worthwhile anymore. He
looked forward to the remaining two years of his term with complete dread.[8] Three months later he told House that he was deeply
lonely and wished someone would kill him. Only his Calvinist sense
of duty kept him going.[9] As his personal crisis developed he fell back
on familiar Presbyterian habits and language: "The duty has been my
salvation,"[10] and "safety lies in having my attention absolutely fixed
elsewhere than upon myself."[11]

House recognized that Ellen's death was a severe loss to the president. Her counsel had been a moderating influence on him. The
colonel allowed himself to lapse into uncharacteristically Calvinist language upon news of her death, describing her as "one of the
elect."[12] For a time House became Wilson's confidant, replacing Ellen
in that role to a small degree. The president could open many of his
inner thoughts to House, and rewarded this reciprocal friendship with

his confidence.[13] In the end, however, Wilson needed a woman's companionship.[14] In March 1915, at the instigation of Grayson and Wilson's cousin Helen Bones, a "chance" meeting took place between the president and Edith Galt, a socially prominent Washington widow. They were married in December.

The president's reaction to Ellen's sickness and death highlighted the pattern of information processing Wilson employed when faced with circumstances that seemed to contradict his presuppositions. He began his decision-making process with a confident, presupposed, providential, inner picture of the truth and an idea about the ultimate outcome of his action. Though clear to him, it was a subjective inner concursus of the competing facts as he saw them. He then subjected his judgments and language to this inner picture. Once a conviction was fixed in his mind, he limited or rejected outside or contradictory information. He read prepared summaries, gave a cursory glance at other material and relied upon verbal reports from those closest to him who often screened out information to keep him unencumbered with detail.[15] His decision processes were kept simple. What information he did get was categorized by how it did or did not fit the picture and outcome upon which he had already settled. When circumstances proved his analysis wrong he responded with shock, as in Ellen's death, or anger and denial, as in political reversals. He would then adjust the new information to the circumstances, refitting this information into his existing providential view of the world and working harder toward the original goal.

Though his wife's death was personal, the process he went through shows a pattern of thinking connected broadly to his world view and his theological patterns. The Princeton Presbyterian theologians who influenced Wilson held optimistic views of the ultimate end of the world. They were held in combination with the present-life focus of Scottish common-sense realism, but they were optimistic about the triumph of the gospel in this age.[16] He developed his conviction about how the international order worked from this confident, progressive, presuppositional eschatology. He developed a view of his and his family's place in this progressive plan of God based in this theology as well. Ellen's death highlighted the manner in which all these threads came together in his mind as he dealt with circumstances that seemed to contradict these preconceptions. It becomes a window into his later handling of contradiction, especially during the treaty negotiations and subsequent battle with the Senate.

In the end, hard work, steadfast faith, and duty had brought Wilson to where he was. He believed it would be enough to get him through. Despair or disappointments would be followed by periods of hard work, devotion to duty, and acceptance that this was part of God's mysterious plan to achieve the promised end, which would bring renewed hope in the final outcome. Those around Wilson marveled at the speed with which he came to conclusions. House commented that his friend had one of the most ordered minds he had met.[17] That was because the president's thought processes followed an internal order based upon his faith and were not complicated by the chaos or detail of the world around him. After processing Ellen's death, he concluded that God had taken his wife but left him because he had not yet accomplished his purpose as divine messenger. The fact that he was still alive worked to strengthen an inner view of his divine mission.

Wilson's approach to international policy during this period was colored by an increasing tendency to personalize the interaction of nations. This tendency had always been present in him. Indeed, to Wilson and his fellow evangelicals, political issues, whether national or international, were just personal issues writ large. Bryan's "Prince of Peace" speech is a classic example.[18] The secretary extrapolated the idea that a personal response to Christ was the key to getting society as a whole to become Christlike in its service to humanity. Wilson's approach to international relations, however, became even more personal following Ellen's death. "Peace will come to the world when we love our fellow man better than we love ourselves."[19] If individuals behaved differently, the international order would change. He became even more invested in his personal mission to create a better world. He treated the world even more like a Presbyterian congregation. His speeches were calls for personal moral reform and conversion stated in international political language. The nation and the world were spoken to and about in the language and imagery of the individual.

At the same time as Wilson was equating national and international politics with the personal, he also tended to identify entire nations with the personalities of their leaders.[20] He read character sketches of the European leaders with great interest and discussed their temperaments with close friends.[21] Having established in his mind the *character* of the national leader, he proceeded to judge the policies of that country, in part, based on those judgments. U.S. response to those countries often reflected his personal like or dislike of the nation's leadership, occasionally baffling diplomats. The fact that Wilson had never actually met these leaders, at least until 1919, but relied upon impressions passed on to him from others, never seemed to bother him.

As the United States became more involved in the European conflict, Bryan became a victim of the president's increased sense of personal mission. Prior to the outbreak of conflict, and in the early months after the war in Europe began, Wilson continued to hold a benign if condescending view of his secretary of state.[22] He had long before categorized Bryan as an intellectual lightweight who would be a liability to the president and to the country should the United States become involved in serious foreign business. Bryan had been useful for taking on unpopular causes from which the president needed or wanted to distance himself. Indeed, he had been a welcome lightning rod in keeping the heat of the more radical progressive reformers away from the president.[23] As the war progressed and the international situation became more complex, however, Bryan's idealistic principles, which seemed unreasonable to Wilson, became an irritation. The secretary had now become an obstacle to God's mission. By December 1914 the president was looking for an issue that would cause Bryan to resign.[24]

Wilson's foreign policy was complicated by the way he approached the meaning of language and written texts. Much of his apparently contradictory attitude when it came to language was derived from his understanding of the nature of written documents. Antinomy created the truth behind the language. Even when he acted in apparent contradiction to the words of a written document, he remained convinced that the document was important and that he was holding to the true meaning. He held to the spirit of the language if not the letter, as some other readers might read it. He failed to see the difference others saw between letter and spirit.

Wilson believed that the true meaning of a written constitution was to be found not in the letter of its text, but rather in some agreed-upon interpretation. Interpretation, and thus true meaning, could change without any change in the text. House noted in his diary: "He began to speak of a flexible or fluid constitution in contradistinction to a rigid one. He thought that constitutions changed without the text being altered, and cited our own as an example."[25] The president argued that the Constitution had granted the states primacy over the union until Andrew Jackson's presidency because the people had interpreted it that way. However, during Jackson's presidency the view of the people changed. The importance that they placed upon the union established its predominance and preempted the right of a state to secede. He tied this to the concept of the power of a messenger to persuade people of the meaning. In *History of the American People* he wrote about Jackson's ability to both embody the will of the people and bring about change.[26] House indicated in his *Diary* that, in his private discussions with Wilson, the president continued to hold this view even as he developed it further. This change in the Constitution was achieved without any change in its text. Wilson was sentimentally attached to the South, an advocate of states rights on many issues, but he was committed to a flexible meaning of the Constitution and thus willing to accept that the meaning of the U.S. Constitution had changed.

As the war in Europe progressed, with increasingly horrifying consequences, Wilson began to interpret laws regarding American neutrality with the same flexibility of meaning. Just as a presbytery of elders or a general assembly could arrive at a new agreed-upon meaning for a scriptural passage without any alteration in its text, so national leaders could determine the meaning of treaties and conventions through deliberation without agreeing on changes in the language of the texts.[27] Providence working through this type of providential messenger caused progress. Resistance to this providential change would leave society behind.

Wilson's thought as the war in Europe began was influenced by a predetermined view of the world, formed by his religion, through which he processed his information about events. He categorized the personalities of the political leaders on a sliding scale between righ-

teous and unrighteous, then interpreted national and international
policies through the lens of his understanding of those personalities.
He held a view of language that involved changeable meaning which
could supercede the literal or original meaning of words and allowed
the understanding of the text to evolve. These patterns of thought
allowed him to retain an optimistic vision of his mission in the world
while interpreting conflicting external evidence in a way that brought
it into conformity with his presupposed view of world order.

On August 3, 1914, as the nations of Europe declared war on each
other, Wilson took a break from sitting with Ellen to type a short letter to House, who had just returned from his unsuccessful mission to
broker peace in Europe. As his own personal world collapsed around
him, the president wrote of his confidence in the ultimate providential
outcome of the chaos. "I know how deep a sorrow must have come
to you out of this dreadful European conflict in view of what we had
hoped the European world was going to turn to, but we must face the
situation in the confidence that providence has deeper plans than we
could possibly have laid to ourselves."[28] As late as November 1914 the
president wrote that "The war in Europe may have been a godsend."[29]
He was unshaken by the conflict since, despite the carnage, it seemed
to open possibilities for his own mission to bring God's order to the
world. He was called by God. The pressure of Ellen's death had not
changed the course already fixed in his mind. Rather, the pressure
brought about by her death and the simultaneous eruption of war
hardened his resolve to work. He need not understand, he need only
be faithful.

The first issue that he had to work through was American neutrality. If he was called to help bring about a peaceful world, then it
was providential that America was neutral, above the fray in Europe.
American neutrality would have to be active, however—it was an integral part of a divine mission. Neutrality would allow him to induce
the warring nations to accept the American government as the honest broker who could help settle their differences. He envisioned the
United States as an active agent in bringing peace and influencing the
postwar world order.

The same purpose that had motivated the sermon Wilson gave
to the graduating Princeton students in 1907 drove his missionary

neutrality as president of the United States: the transformation of the world to conform to a heavenly pattern.[30] In that address he spoke of the conquering spirit of Christ who would go with the Princeton graduates. From Romans 12 he challenged them to "be not conformed to the world but transformed" that they in turn could transform the world. They were to be "born again" if they were to truly live. His challenge to them was that as men with a mission to the world they should, like Christ, mediate between the two worlds of the present age and the age to come. Illuminating his views on the interpretation of texts and the mission of the messenger, and previewing the attitude he wished to take toward active neutrality, Wilson turned to the example of Jesus:

> And if Christ is adjusted to all ages he is conformed to none: he is the only true citizen of the world. There is in him constant renewal, the fresh, undying quality that draws always direct from the sources of knowledge and of conduct. He interprets,—only he can perfectly interpret,—our text. His is the non-conformity of the perfect individual, unsophisticated, unstaled, unsubdued. . . . Not all the hoarded counsel of the world is worth the example of a single person: it is abstract, intangible until incarnated: and here, incarnate, is the man Christ who in his life and person shows us and all the world "what is that good, and acceptable, and perfect will of God."[31]

His language as president was more moderated for his political audience, but the mission was unmistakably the same. The president's first public response to the war, on August 18, 1914, shortly after he returned from burying Ellen, explained and justified neutrality in these activist terms. America was holding itself "ready to play a part of impartial mediation. . . ." It was a "nation fit beyond others . . . ," that "keeps herself fit and free to do what is necessary and disinterested and truly serviceable for the peace of the world."[32] This first statement reiterated the "redeemer nation" aspect of Wilson's thought. It also expressed the policy of activist neutrality he intended to follow as the war in Europe progressed. Providence had put into the hands of America and its president the opportunity to accomplish the mandate to bring peace to the world.

America was neutral in this fight. This gave it the ability, indeed duty, to act. Wilson believed the United States was not only above partisanship, but so far above it that the belligerents would have to recognize American objectivity and good will. This was, of course, what he had believed regarding the factions in Mexico, what he likely still believed of them. It was a neutrality in the service of the good. It was a neutrality that allowed America to act on behalf of the righteous. Once again the president's presuppositional approach to information affected his foreign policy. From the beginning of the conflict there was a bias in the administration toward Britain and against Germany. Wilson was predisposed to be an Anglophile. He admired British political institutions. His Presbyterianism came from the British Isles. Britain was the historical source of the American people's divine sense of purpose toward the world. This view of Britain caused Wilson to interpret information in a way that favored British interests and penalized Germany while continuing to believe that he and the country were being absolutely neutral.

Trying to maintain the integrity of American neutrality, as he defined it, the president did attempt to keep the appearance of balance toward both sides. He directed American Ambassador to Germany James Gerard to avoid anti-German statements, while at the same time he cautioned his ambassador to Britain, Walter Hines Page, about his inflammatory pro-British notes home.[33] But the reality of the bias was evident. Gerard had to be cautioned to try to avoid insulting his host, Page had to be cautioned to remember he represented the U.S. and not Britain. The president viewed politics as relationships, and the choices for ambassador to Britain and Germany had reflected his bias. Wilson felt warmly toward his friend Page and the British and disliked and distrusted Germany and his ambassador Gerard, describing him to Edith Galt as an "ass" and an "idiot" in a note in the margin of his dispatches which he passed on to her to read.[34] Subsequent attempts at "strict neutrality" further highlighted his prejudice against Germany.

Wilson had developed these prejudices on many levels. The Princeton theologians he knew and respected expressed deep concerns about "German theology," which became a kind of coded term for "infidelity to the truth." Though over time they had accepted many of the particulars of German theology at Princeton, the bad reputation and feeling toward it remained.[35] Wilson translated his caution about German thought into a broad judgment about German politi-cal philosophy. He described it as "selfish and lacking in spirituality."[36] The essence of sin in Wilson's Calvinism was selfishness.[37] It was this selfishness which he believed he had battled within himself all his life. Following Ellen's death he was particularly aware of the tendency to focus on self which grief could produce. He described his presiden-tial duty as his salvation because it forced him to avoid this danger.[38] Describing the Germans as "selfish and unspiritual" meant, in his Presbyterian language, that they were evil. The German leaders and thinkers served themselves, and in doing so served the cause of Satan and resisted the mission of God and his messengers.

Another level of the president's bias against the Germans was motivated by his perception that they did not honor covenants. House recorded that Wilson was indignant "at the German Chancellor's des-ignation of the Belgian Treaty as being 'only a scrap of paper.'"[39] His thinking about the text and the spirit allowed him to believe that the text meant what people agreed it meant, and thus was fluid. But he also believed that texts themselves were sacred, the essential starting point for coming to this covenantal understanding. Whether scrip-ture or treaties, texts were not mere "scraps of paper." To change the meaning of a written covenant by mutual informed agreement was progress. To disregard the text itself was a literal desecration. It was like calling the Bible a scrap of paper.

The administration's effort to secure general adoption of the Dec-laration of London, an unratified 1909 convention on international maritime law, demonstrates this antinomy in regard to texts and their interpretation. Wilson insisted that Britain publicly endorse the unratified Declaration. The British refused to do so, as they did not intend to follow it. Wilson's position was that if they would publicly honor the text of the declaration they would be free to make supple-mentary statements of interpretation that would loosen the restric-tions they found objectionable. Lansing made it quite clear to Page that if the British publicly adopted the Declaration, they would be left free to interpret it in accordance with circumstances as they arose.[40] The text provided the basis for agreement, but interpretation of the text was flexible. While the text was fixed, the meaning, the interpre-tation, progressed as the parties negotiated. The president was fully engaged in the negotiation between the State Department and the British government.[41]

The pronouncements on neutrality also underwent change and reinterpretation. By April 1915 the president had begun to spell out his policy of active neutrality. On April 20, in remarks to the Associated Press, he spoke of putting "America first." This, he explained, was not a selfish idea. It could not be, because selfishness was sin. Rather, putting America first was inherently unselfish because America was not a mere nation but a noble ideal. The United States was divinely chosen to be the "mediating nation of the world."[42] Such biblical language had always been the foundation of Wilson's thought. It was the eschatological language of Isaiah 2 and Micah 4, which Bryan had inscribed on miniature plowshares (the text in italics below), beaten out from melted U.S. cavalry swords. These were subsequently delivered as gifts to embassies around the world:

> The mountain of the LORD's house shall be established in the top of the mountains, and shall be exalted above the hills; and all nations shall flow unto it. Come, let us go up to the mountain of the Lord, to the house of the God of Jacob; and he will teach us of his ways, and we will walk in his paths: for out of Zion shall go forth the law, and the word of the LORD from Jerusalem. And he shall judge among the nations, and shall rebuke many people: and *they shall beat their swords into plowshares*, and their spears into pruninghooks: nation shall not lift up sword against nation, neither shall they learn war any more.[43]

The language of his April press conference embodied Wilson's religious thought, the personal sense of mission he felt, and the redeemer nation image he held of the United States. The nation was not neutral because it was afraid of righteous conflict, it was neutral because it had a greater destiny than war. Destined by God and under godly leadership it would lead the world to the promised land of peace and prosperity.[44]

Wilson perceived the American situation in 1914 as parallel to the War of 1812. He often compared the two situations in private and in public, as he did in a speech to the Chamber of Commerce in Columbus, Ohio.[45] He wished to avoid the trap Madison had fallen into—which, according to Wilson's interpretation of history, had been going to war with Britain while the great threat to civilization had been Napoleon. This time the United States would use its power as an aggressive neutral to conquer the forces of disorder and selfishness in the world on all sides. America would use its special status to create and enforce a peace that would give rise to a better system of international behavior. The president referred to his policy of neutrality as the "peaceful conquest of the world."[46]

Wilson pursued neutrality with the object of creating, or at least being a major influence on, the international system that would follow the war. Believing that the war would leave two powers dominating world politics, the United States and Russia,[47] Wilson and House discussed ways to fuse the Western hemisphere together in a democratic alliance, dominated by the United States, which could compel this new international system.[48] American neutrality had international purpose.

The president grew more confident in the role of divine messenger as he continued to face the challenges of the war. He was not hesitant about blending faith with his position, and worried little about separating his personal religion from his actions in office. When a false report circulated in the press that he had led the Cabinet in prayer seeking divine guidance in the difficult times, he did not distance himself from the sentiment but instead responded: "I am sorry to say that this incident is not true. I wish that it were."[49]

House was a master at reading Wilson and adapting his own ideas and language to reflect presidential views. In November 1915 he spoke of the great role Wilson had the opportunity to play upon the international stage. "This is the part I think you are destined to play in this world tragedy, and it is the noblest part that has ever come to a son of man."[50] House employed the same language of predestination, mission, and duty that Wilson used about himself. The phrase, *son of man*, though referring generically to any human being, was normally used in scripture when a prophet was referring to himself. In the New Testament, in all but one passage, it referred to Christ. Wilson had appropriated this language, in the prophetic sense, to refer to himself. In response to a challenge to his stance on American preparedness a few days before the House "son of man" letter, the president quoted Ezekiel: "Son of man, speak unto the children of thy people."[51] He explicitly compared himself to the prophet and the watchman described in the passage. House used this language, though it was unusual for him, understanding how it would register with Wilson. At that time, the president refrained from comparing himself to Christ. Later, during the treaty fight, even this comparison was employed.

Wilson, like many nineteenth-century American leaders, equated the United States with God's chosen people in his speeches. He extrapolated from that equation an American mission to evangelize the world politically. He equated patriotism with Christianity. "Patriotism in its redeeming quality resembles Christianity. . . . It makes [a man] forget himself and square every thought and action with something infinitely greater than himself."[52] To the Chamber of Commerce in Columbus, Ohio, he had spoken about the "peaceful conquest of the world" through "spiritual mediation."[53] He clarified this assertion in a speech to the Gridiron Club on December 11, 1915. That conquest was to be accomplished by conquering the "spirit of the world."[54] This is the language of conversion, taken from the concepts in his early speech "Christ's Army," which still organized his view of the world. He was a preacher calling the nation and the world to repentance. Neutrality as defined by international law was too passive a concept to express what Wilson meant.[55] The neutrality of the United States would conquer, convert, and change the nations: "the world cannot resist the moral force of great triumphant convictions."[56]

Wilson negotiated the antinomy created in his mind by this active neutrality with a series of initiatives and statements that seemed to bounce between preparedness and pacifism. He criticized Germany for building a military machine ostensibly in the name of peace. "What a foolish thing it was to create a powder magazine and risk someone's dropping a spark into it."[57] He resisted pressure to prepare for possible military conflict, especially by building a "large army."[58] On the other hand the more passive, defensive, neutrality that Bryan advocated irritated Wilson. He said it was "unreasonable."[59] His active neutrality was a peacemaking endeavor, not pacifism. He sought to find ways to *increase* the military short of building this "large army," ways that would make the United States more effective in its peacemaking mission. He supported measures designed to beef up reserve forces and modernize the military, such as the Navy bill approved by congress on August 29, 1916.[60]

In the left margin, handwritten: *arming small milit small*

In speeches on "Preparedness" throughout 1915 and early 1916 the president tried to keep his balance between the pacifists and militarists. He justified an increase in military spending, arguing that it was purely for defense. In many ways his words matched the policy advocated by Bryan, but the president had larger plans than his secretary of state. The nation was chosen for the mission of making a better world. He had no intention of arming the country, as the European powers had done, for selfish reasons. The United States would resist militarist passions, while preparing for its mission.[61] The country was not preparing for war by strengthening its armed forces, rather, it was making itself strong to be the "spiritual mediator" of the better covenant. America was not a "powder keg."[62] Activist neutrality proved to be a difficult antinomy to maintain, but maintain it he must.

Events in Europe continued to complicate Wilson's position on neutrality. On May 7, 1915 a German U-boat torpedoed the British liner *Lusitania,* killing 128 Americans. The German action horrified Wilson. He spent the next two days in seclusion from the public, going to church, reading dispatches, composing a response to Germany, and visiting only with his family and Mrs. Galt.[63] House wired Wilson from England that "an immediate demand should be made upon Germany." House wanted a declaration of war or at least an ultimatum threatening war. Germany should be informed that "our government should be expected to take whatever measures were necessary." He went on to say that "we can no longer remain neutral spectators . . . We are being weighed in the balance, and our position amongst the nations is being assessed by mankind."[64] Bryan, on the other hand, encouraged the president to ban Americans from taking passage on ships also carrying munitions, as the *Lusitania* had been.[65] Other public and political leaders pressed for the United States to assert its right to trade with Europe even at the risk of war.[66] On Monday, May 10th, Wilson went to work on the U.S. response. He retained the antinomy between these contending views, but the emotion of the situation took its toll. As he worked on his response, he became definite, more fixed in his view, less tolerant and more suspicious of those who were putting pressure on him from either side of the issue. When a telegram arrived at the White House saying "in the name of God and humanity declare war on Germany," he responded that "war isn't declared in the name of God, it is a human affair entirely."[67]

Though angry with those who were pushing for war, he had lost his patience with the pacifists as well. The first note to Germany was only reluctantly signed by Bryan. The second note was too strong and the secretary of state refused to sign it. The note provided the opportunity for the break with Bryan that the president told House he was looking for months earlier. By June 5th, with the second *Lusitania* note to Germany, the breach was complete. Bryan resigned on June 9th. Wilson told Mrs. Galt that he considered Bryan a traitor for leaving the administration, despite his desire to be rid of Bryan. The outgoing secretary was more perceptive: "Colonel House has been Secretary of State, not I, and I have never had your full confidence."[68]

Pacifist and militarist impulses were both growing in the country. Wilson continued to try to keep them under control. If war became a necessity it must be a peacemaking war. In Philadelphia, on May 10th, he made his first public address following the *Lusitania* incident. To a crowd that included a large number of newly naturalized citizens, he spoke of America's mission to the world. His eloquence was often at its peak when he was under pressure. He told the crowd that by swearing allegiance to the United States they were swearing allegiance to no one except, perhaps, God.[69] America was not the people who governed but an ideal, a great body of principles. Like the president who was speaking to them, they were committing themselves to a higher cause, something greater than a mere great power. They would need to find in this commitment their own internal antinomy formed by the interaction of these principles. Presumably that antinomy would mirror that of their president.

Wilson used biblical imagery and cadence as he preached to his new congregants. They had come because of this faith. They hoped for that which they believed in. They were dreamers of dreams and motivated by the vision which their faith and hope had produced.[70] His revival-style speech culminated:

> The example of America must be the example, not merely of peace because it will not fight, but of peace because peace is the healing and elevating influence of the world, and strife is not. There is such a thing

as a man being too proud to fight. There is such a thing as a nation being so right that it does not need to convince others by force that it is right.[71]

Later, when sent a transcript of this speech to be published, Wilson deleted the "too proud to fight" sentence entirely. Yet it may be a better reflector of his views than the official version edited when his passions cooled. The speech reflected his optimistic Calvinism. The nation, like an elect individual, was willing to do the right thing even if it meant suffering abuse and scorn for that right. America was the "house of the Lord" in prophetic imagery, the "city on a hill" of the Puritan founders. Its leader was fulfilling his divinely appointed mission. The pressures from either side were not going to knock him off his righteous course.

Lansing, who replaced Bryan as secretary of state, represented a different, perhaps some would say a more realistic, strand of Presbyterianism, unwashed by the thinking of the idealistic Princeton divines and more prone to see fallen human nature in the behavior of nations. He wrote in his diary: "I do not recall a case in history in which a nation surrendered its sovereignty for the sole purpose of being right."[72] Unimpressed by the president's higher ideals, he wrote that

> [I]ntuition rather than reason played the chief part in the way in which he reached conclusions and judgements. In fact, arguments, however soundly reasoned, did not appeal to him if they were opposed to his feeling of what was the right thing to do. Even established facts were ignored if they did not fit in with his intuitive sense, this semi-divine power to select the right.[73]

Complaining that Wilson never doubted his judgments he went on to say: "How did he know they were right? Why he *knew* it, and that was the best reason in the world. . . . When reason clashed with his intuition, reason had to give way."[74]

Lansing, believing he should deal with the persistent, unyielding facts of the world as it existed, could not appreciate the inner antinomy of Wilson's mind. Adding to the sense of irony growing in Lansing was the fact that the president seemed to lack any self-awareness of how his manner of thought and leadership style came across to others. A speech by the president December 10, 1914, to the Federal Council of Churches, could have described himself:

An egotist is a man who has got the whole perspective of life wrong. He conceives of himself as the center of affairs even as effects the providence of God. He has not related himself to the great forces which dominate him with the rest of us, and, therefore, has set up a little kingdom all his own in which he reigns with unhonored sovereignty. . . . a life that leads to all sorts of shipwreck. Whatever our doctrine be, our life is conformed to it.[75]

Wilson's confidential relationship with House had competition—it was being replaced by that between Wilson and his new wife, Edith Galt, who grew to distrust House and his closeness to the president.[76] The growing distance between the president and his friend, who was now spending much of his time in Europe, can be detected in House's diaries during this time.[77] Though he was not yet aware of the depth of the replacement, he was increasingly outside the president's thought processes. Away from the president and unable to talk through his antinomies, House misread the intentions of the administration toward the European war. He told the Allied leaders that the United States would intervene militarily should the Allies have a setback on the battlefield.[78] This was a stronger assertion than was warranted by the correspondence between himself and the president.[79] There was no indication in their letters that Wilson was pursuing any plan other than active neutrality when he spoke about intervention based upon the "highest human motives."[80] But House, across the Atlantic, read the president's correspondence to mean military intervention. The breach between the two had not yet come but the signs were there.

By December 20, 1916, faced with the reluctance of the president to commit the U.S. military, House complained bitterly: "the president has nearly destroyed all the work I have done in Europe."[81] The president could not have known of this concern since House expressed it subtly, buried in flowery language about the president's mission and role in the new world they were building.[82] Here is where the capacity of the fluid meaning of texts to engender confusion began to show in the administration's policy. Wilson, House, and Lansing used the same words about neutrality and intervention, but held different meanings. For Wilson, the words were connected to his internal concursus of activism and neutrality. Meanwhile, House acted on his interpretation of the president's words. When he did so it caused Wilson great frustration, his impatience fueled by his wife, who felt that her counsel was best. During this time he began to grow concerned about the clarity of his friend's principles. Eventually the president, encouraged by Edith, would question House's honesty, courage, and loyalty as well.

For the time being, however, the president's words seemed to vacillate between peace and war. In December 1915 he spoke of a "peace with guarantees," a world in which "law not power would rule." To achieve this, America would intervene with a "spiritual mediation."[83] Hoping to do something new in the history of international politics, the president spoke of both law and spirit, a combination that in his mind meant something quite different than *law* as Lansing, a practicing lawyer, would have understood it.

On May 27, 1916 Wilson gave an address to the League to Enforce Peace. He said that the United States had no interest in the causes of the war. What was of interest to it was how to bring about a new international order that would prevent this sort of bloody conflict from happening in the future. He talked of a world where "coercion would no longer be used in the service of political ambition or selfish hostility, but service of common order, common justice, common peace."[84] This new order would require the *spiritual mediation* of the United States. If necessary the new system would use force, as the U.S. had been forced to do in Mexico, Haiti, and the Dominican Republic, but it would be *neutral* force to mediate peace. God's messenger would drive out the money changers, enabling the poor and downtrodden to find a better world. The address, which lacked any specifics, seemed clear to the president. It nevertheless confused both the advocates of peace and the advocates of military intervention. Both felt unclear as to the president's intentions. When a group of Chicago ministers wrote to him with encouragement to keep America at peace, Wilson responded with Ezekiel 33:6: "But if the watchman see the sword come and blow not the trumpet, and the people be not warned, if the sword come, and take any person from among them . . . his blood will I require at the watchman's hand."[85] This must have seemed to them as clear as dirt.

Looking for avenues to use the mediating offices of the United States, Wilson sent a diplomatic communiqué requesting that the belligerent nations declare their war aims. What specifically would it take for them to be able to determine that the war was over?[86] His antinomy in regard to American neutrality finally found expression in his "peace without victory" address to the Senate. It did not express a particularly new idea. On December 14, 1914 he had said that "the chance of a just and equitable peace, and of the only possible peace that will be lasting, will be the happiest if no nation gets the decision by arms."[87] But to the Senate on January 22, 1917, he spelled it out more clearly when he said:

> [I]t must be a peace without victory. It is not pleasant to say this. I beg that I may be permitted to put my own interpretation upon it and that it may be understood that no other interpretation was in my thought. I am seeking only to face realities and to face them without soft concealments. Victory would mean peace forced upon the loser, a victor's terms imposed upon the vanquished. It would be accepted in humiliation, under duress, at an intolerable sacrifice, and would leave a sting, a resentment, a bitter memory upon which terms of peace would rest, not permanently, but only as upon quicksand. Only a peace between equals can last.[88]

The battle for the conquest of the "spirit of the world" had begun.

World events quickly forced Wilson to renegotiate this inner providential picture. On January 31, 1917 Germany announced unrestricted submarine warfare. On February 3rd the United States broke diplomatic relations with Germany. On February 28th the Zimmerman telegram, encouraging Mexico to retake its land in the southwestern United States and promising German support, was published.[89] Public outcry against Germany in the United States was overwhelming. The president's sense of justice could no longer support even active neutrality. On April 2, 1917 before a joint session of Congress he asked for a declaration of war. Demonstrating the utter perseverance of his vision—to the bafflement of both contemporaries and historians—Wilson continued to speak of the same principles that he had espoused up to this time, ideas like peace without victory and spiritual mediation. Now, however, the *spiritual mediation* of the United States would work in antinomy with the steel and lead of the military. He closed the speech with a phrase reminiscent of Martin Luther at the Diet of Worms: "America is privileged to spend her exceptionalism?

blood and her might for the principles that gave her birth and the happiness and the peace which she has treasured. God helping her, she can do no other."[90] For Wilson, this war was still about peace. It was still about a new order. He continued to believe that America was above the fray even as American soldiers were killing and dying in Europe. If not literally neutral, it remained neutral in spirit, which always represented the higher, more persistent, reality to Woodrow Wilson.

Over the nine months following the declaration of war the president worked to redefine America's providential role. He must make this a righteous war. That internal renegotiation culminated in the Fourteen Points address which he delivered to Congress on January 8, 1918.[91] Using a Christ analogy, the points could be considered his "sermon on the mount" applied to international relations. Or perhaps they were, as French Premier Georges Clemenceau alluded to them, more akin to Moses' tablets of stone. Either way, the president had found a righteous cause for the United States to fight in. For Wilson, the Fourteen Points raised the stakes, creating a situation in which it was absolutely essential that one idea win and the other lose. There was no middle ground on the points. He was now, finally, leading Christ's army in the battle that he had written about so long ago. It would be a hard fought battle in which the great forces of evil would "quail before the uplifted swords of the Spirit." There was no place for compromise on principle. "For there is no middle course, no neutrality. Each one must enlist either with the followers of Christ or those of Satan."[92] Standing before the joint session of Congress he said:

> We have spoken now. . . . An evident principle runs through the whole programme I have outlined. It is the principle of justice to all peoples and nationalities, and their right to live on equal terms of liberty and safety with one another, whether they be strong or weak. Unless this principle be made its foundation no part of the structure of international justice can stand. . . . The moral climax of this [is that] the culminating and final war for human liberty has come.[93]

A final war, a new system, a better covenant between the nations were at stake. There was no turning back. The providential time had come to make a better world.

4

Negotiating the Tablets of Stone

The end of the war came suddenly and with profound implications for Wilson's sense of divine mission. On October 6, 1918 he received a communication from the German government via the Swiss chargé d'affaires asking for peace based upon the Fourteen Points address.[1] The president responded to the Germans. This was great news for the Americans. Finally, Wilson would be in the role of mediator he had sought for so long. Delighted, he came into the cabinet meeting of October 8th whistling.[2] On October 16th he informed the head of British intelligence in the United States, Sir William Wiseman, that the United States was prepared to accept the offer. He again insisted that the Fourteen Points and the League of Nations "should be the very centre [sic] of the Peace agreement. The pillars upon which the house should rest."[3]

Though there were many causes for the end of the fighting, it is not difficult to see how the president would attribute a large part to his own influence in world events. It was a chain of events that seemed to correspond to his own efforts. Wilson was amazed and deeply encouraged as he watched. On October 23rd he accepted the German offer to discuss an armistice while at the same time appealing to them to reorganize their government so that it would be constitutionally responsible to the German people.[4] On October 28th the German constitution was altered to create a constitutional monarchy. Throughout October, Wilson and House also pressured the Allied leaders to accept American mediation, at one time threatening a separate peace if they would not accept in principle the Fourteen Points as the basis for negotiation. Britain and France had no choice but to accept. They agreed with certain reservations, which was good enough for Wilson. A few days later the German navy mutinied, forcing the resignation of the German chancellor and installing a Socialist government. On November 6th, the new government sent formal peace emissaries and on November 11th, the Armistice was signed. The United States had become the central player in mediating the new peace in Europe, and Wilson's "words" were to be the basis of that peace.

These apparent presidential influences on the end of the war and the reorganization of the German government seemed further evidence to the president of his divine mission, another "Providential timing." The peace appeared to provide him the opportunity to put into effect that which he had been elected by God to do. On November 18th, changing his mind about sending House to head the negotiation team, he announced that he would personally lead the American delegation to Paris.[5] He was going, he said, because the American people would approve of this errand and also because he would have to be involved directly in the "greater outlines of the final treaty."[6] He was pursuing a divine cause.[7]

Both House and Lansing felt that the decision to go to Paris in person was a mistake.[8] House was concerned about a loss of prestige, as the president would be reduced to just one member of the committee. Lansing privately mused that Wilson would find it difficult to "step down from his pedestal" and negotiate as an equal with European leaders.[9] Yet the president was determined to see his project through. He had grown increasingly frustrated at the failure of those around him to see the antinomy of his internal logic. A year earlier he had assured House that of all his administration only the colonel could represent him: "No one in America, or in Europe either, knows my mind and I am not willing to trust them to attempt to interpret it."[10] While he had been willing to send House as his representative to the early Armistice negotiations, telling Wiseman, "He knows my mind entirely,"[11] by this time he was not. It seemed to the president that House was not up to the task of interpreting the finer points of the principles Wilson was pressing the Europeans for, much less reconciling the contradictions into a simple unity as Wilson was capable of doing. The president was personally called by God to a mission. He could no longer trust anyone else to do it correctly. Duty, spiritual and material, bound him to go to Paris. The dire predictions of some of his advisors about the dangers of his going in person did not concern him. His divine destiny would overcome these new obstacles to his vision as it had overcome previous obstacles in his life.

World events continued to encourage Wilson to view himself as a man on a divine mission. House's communication to Wilson, far from dampening this sense of personal mission, made the president even more sure that he must go. Following the Wilsons' arrival in Paris, even House seemed persuaded that the decision had been right. Thirty-six thousand French soldiers held back the nearly hysterical crowds as Wilson traveled from Brest to Paris. After the president's arrival House met with British newspaper owner Lord Northcliff and "got him to admit" that "[T]he Entente Governments as now constituted could not interpret the aspirations of the peoples of their respective countries and . . . Wilson was the only statesman who could do so."[12] As a result of this meeting House worked on a publicity campaign which he convinced the president to launch with an interview in England. In conversation and in letter he assured the president that he had a historic destiny. He referred to him as the "son of man," sending articles which hailed Wilson as the hero of a new international order. An article by Gustave Hervé from *La Victoire* of March 7, 1917, enclosed in one note, referred to the president as one day presiding over the "Congress of Nations" which through his hard work was "founded as upon a rock."[13] Hervé called him the "shepherd of the people."[14]

This Christlike imagery clearly resonated with Wilson. A poem written by Edward Park Davis compared his second inauguration to the second coming of Christ:

He stood upon the eastern gate,
Behind him rose the pillared dome . . .
His speech was voice of human man,
His thoughts the words of living God.[15]

The long poem was filled with comparisons to Christ and Christian eschatological references. The president was "David," the "High Priest," "God's voice" in the earth, the one "before whose march oppression falls," and other images of the triumphant return of Christ. Wilson wrote Davis that his poem had "touched me more than I know how to say. I read it aloud to Mrs. Wilson and Miss Bones. . . . I owe you, my dear fellow, a real debt of gratitude for the encouragement you have given me."[16] Cooper has written that Wilson's clerical family background would have kept him from having any delusions about being a messianic crusader in politics.[17] Yet upon looking at this evidence there can be little doubt that by the end of the war the relentless pursuit of his mission, the obstacles he had overcome, the encouragement of those around him, and the influence on world events which his office allowed, caused him, at the very least, to entertain such views of himself.

The Europeans, however, complicated his mission to save the world. Prior to Wilson's arrival in Paris the Allies put forward a proposal to form a league of their own. This seemed common sense to the European leaders. Their countries had been negotiating international treaties for centuries. American involvement in the various Hague Conventions in the decades preceding the war had been helpful, but the nations of Europe had not planned to cede their traditional role of leadership.[18] Indeed they did not yet see that they had need to. So they set about doing what they had always done, putting together a new set of treaties and alliances. Once they had this structure in place they would return to business as usual. This league would be put together by the victorious Europeans and include their American associates. Neutrals and others would be invited to join at the discretion of the victorious nations.

This European plan for "business as usual" disturbed the president. It was important to Wilson that the right group of founding nations create the league. The members of this league must be committed to a new way of doing international politics. The nations who signed the treaty must have enough conviction about those principles to give up their old selfish ambitions. The belligerents on either side lacked this commitment. "The principle is easy to adhere to, but the moment questions of organization are taken up all sorts of jealousies come to the front."[19] Any league must have the president of the United States involved or it would be the old business with a new name. The crowds in Europe seemed to agree with Wilson. This time the United States was not going to be a junior partner in the discussions. American power was still intact. Public opinion was on Wilson's side in Europe. The signs were there, for those who wished to see them, that the American century had arrived.

House shared Wilson's concern about the European allies forming their own league. Such an organization would simply become another set of entangling alliances with different groups vying with each other to get neutrals to join their alliance.[20] Wilson was convinced that the Allies, left to themselves, would subvert the mission he had been given and squander the great sacrifice that had been made in the war. Returning to the task versus organization antinomy that he had developed in his thinking early in his life he decided that he must press the Europeans to agree upon the founding principles or the organization would not be the servant of the task of world peace as he envisioned it. These "words without substance," as Keynes called them, would be the foundation of the organization that would change the way international relations was handled.

Lansing believed that Wilson's attitude changed upon his arrival in France. The president's private speech seemed less confident than it had been before, but the cheering crowds in the streets led him to think himself able to accomplish anything.[21] In fact, what Lansing interpreted as Wilson's lack of confidence in private conversations was his growing distrust in the capacity of those around him to fully grasp the "greater principles" which motivated him as he worked to accomplish his mission. In Europe, the president continued to evince the manner of decision making that had characterized him before his arrival. He made decisions with little or no consultation. But now he became, as Lansing noted, even more exclusive, his own repository for all information, opinions, and speculation to which no one else had access. The American delegation was not consulted in the decision-making process. What was even worse, the members were forced to rely on leaks from the staffs of the British and French delegations to learn their own government's position on the issues they were trying to help negotiate.[22] It was not a lack of confidence which afflicted Wilson at this point but a deepening confidence in himself alone, an inner focus on his mission, one that he increasingly felt only he could accomplish. His sense of divine election and his position at the center of world politics came together to create feeling that he could not confide in anyone regarding his task.

fueled by compassion for war torn

redeemer terms

Adding an emotional logic to the image of himself as redeemer of the nations and "shepherd of the people" was Wilson's sincere compassion for the war-ravaged inhabitants of Europe. This sympathy was deeply rooted in him by his Christian faith and his experience as a youth growing up in the post-Civil War South. As the one chosen to be president of the United States at this moment in history, he could do great good for the downtrodden inhabitants of the world. This impulse had been part of the underlying justification for the intervention in Mexico. Now he could help people living under bad governments, feed the hungry, cloth the naked. This became further evidence of his election by God and gave him even greater determination to fulfill his mission. While rejecting salvation by character, Presbyterians like Wilson acknowledged character and good works as evidence of faith. With the other evidence—the influence he had on world events, the challenges he had overcome to arrive at this place, the frenzied crowds that greeted him in Europe—this tangible action of "feeding the multitude" with his war relief efforts made the already-present impulse to view himself in redeemer terms more acute. To Herbert Hoover, head of relief efforts throughout war-torn Europe, he remarked: "a preacher said the Lord's Prayer began with 'Give us this day our daily bread' and said no man could worship God on an empty stomach. Similarly hunger will bring on bolshevikism [*sic*] and anarchy."[23] Mixed with fears about atheist bolshevism was the sense that he was the answer to the Lord's Prayer even for the distressed and defeated German people. He had been used to liberate them from their own oppressive government; now he would secure their future as an integral part of a prosperous, democratic, righteous world.

Wilson was convinced that the popular opinion of the world, which he represented, would win the day. Should that popular opinion fail to convince the European leaders, American economic power would force them to accept the Fourteen Points and the League and Covenant of Nations.[24] He went to Europe prepared for the kind of battle for righteousness that he had espoused twenty years before in "Christ's Army." "I want to go into the peace conference armed with as many weapons as my pockets will hold so as to compel justice."[25] He increasingly spoke like a lone crusader. His language and actions demonstrated that he was not just isolated from his aides and advisors, but that he held himself aloof from the other allied leaders as well. He believed himself to be motivated by a different set of ideals. He was prepared to battle alone if necessary to persuade the European leaders to embrace these greater principles.

Wilson continued to speak of "peace without victory." He was not willing to accept that this concept was not workable after one side won the war. He persisted in advancing this idea even after his own intervention had given the Allies success on the battlefield. Now, instead of mediating a peace between weary belligerents, he found himself in the position of trying to rein in the vindictive impulses of the triumphant side. Ironically, winning the war had weakened Wilson's position on the peace. He soon discovered that he had less compelling weapons in his "pockets" than he had hoped. His tendency to view rhetoric as reality was again demonstrated on this issue. He had spelled out his principle in a series of addresses to Congress and the nation. He continued to believe that his words could create a reality: a reality that the messy ebb and flow of the current international situation unfortunately did not reflect.

To the European leaders the Versailles negotiations should have been a continuation of the international diplomacy which had been underway for over a century, beginning with the Congress of Vienna and more recently the first and second Hague conferences, 1899 and 1907. But the world had taken a sharp turn as a consequence of the destructive war that had just been fought and the addition of a powerful new non-European force, the United States.[26] It would also be changed by the addition of Wilson's vision of how the world ought to be and his faith that it could indeed be made to fit that vision. The president repudiated what he identified as the system of international politics created by the Congress of Vienna.[27] He seemed to have also repudiated, or at least discounted, the work of the Hague conferences of 1899 and 1907. He made little or no mention of them in his own plan.[28] He was willing to take some ideas from the past but had his own idea, the centerpiece of which was the League of Nations. This kind of system was one that he was used to. In some ways his international vision looked like a weaker version of the United States, with the exception of some institutions, like the World Court. He outlined a series of ideas that he felt were interrelated in "peace without victory."

Peace would be accomplished, not merely by war weariness, but by a broad alliance which would supercede the old entangled network of balance-of-power alliances. This new system would be based upon the broader principles of love of justice and right.[29] It would do away with the very need for balance of power—which was based upon fear, not love—replacing the multiple alliances with a single alliance which would eventually include all the nations of the earth. It was an alliance for peace rather than a commitment to go to war. Lansing, upon reading the president's draft in Paris called it "crude" and lacking in any understanding of the already existent Hague conventions.[30]

To reinforce these ideas Wilson downplayed the clauses in the league covenant which implied the use of force, such as Article Ten. Those critics who pointed out potential military entanglements abroad under the covenant were, in his view, missing its entire point.[31] There would be no wars for selfish purposes in the new alliance. All wars would be fought against war. Military conflicts, should they arise, would be peacemaking crusades. The dilemma of what happened when national right met national right would no longer arise. Eventually the national leaders at Paris were able to convince Wilson where his aides had not. South African Jan C. Smuts, Lord Robert Cecil, and others were able to show the president that some of the Hague provisions should be included in the final treaty. Particularly they were able to convince Wilson to include Article Fourteen:

> The Council shall formulate and submit to the Members of the League for adoption plans for the establishment of a Permanent Court of International Justice. The Court shall be competent to hear and determine any dispute of an international character which the parties thereto submit to it. The Court may also give an advisory opinion upon any dispute or question referred to it by the Council or by the Assembly.[32]

This was designed, they convinced Wilson, to handle these very issues of right colliding with right. It was advisory and democratically responsive enough to avoid the danger of becoming hostage to lawyers' thinking, which would have been the kiss of death for Wilson's support.

The nations in the league would work those issues out fairly. Neutrality and isolation would become obsolete. The principle he was fighting for, peace without victory, created a reality that was more tangible for Wilson than the troubling fact that a military victory had already been won. He told a group of newspaper correspondents that he believed in peace without victory more strongly following the signing of the Armistice than he had before.[33] Peace without victory would be the spirit of the final settlement, the manner in which the victors would treat the vanquished. The technical fact that one side had actually won, and would write the peace terms with little input from the defeated, was a minor detail that could not alter the principle. This new system was so different from what had preceded it that Wilson often challenged his listeners not to call it an "alliance." It was more than an alliance. The league was a deliberative body of sovereign nations bound by moral principles, not legal inflexibility. These principles, like those found in the U.S. Constitution, would create a peaceful world order based upon the rule of a higher law than the old alliance systems had been able to create.[34]

Challenges to his principles created by the messy and inconvenient world that existed in the aftermath of the war continued to encroach on Wilson's attention. European leaders made public pronouncements contrary to his understanding of the peace he believed they had agreed upon. He was forced to entertain options to counter this European "selfishness." If Britain and France did not show good faith in his idea of a just peace, he threatened to withdraw from the peace conference and make a separate peace with Germany.[35] He chafed at the seeming hypocrisy of the British who, after agreeing to the Fourteen Points and the principle of disarmament, announced publicly that they intended to retain naval supremacy. He told reporters that if they should try, the "United States could and would build the greatest Navy in the World."[36]

Determined to get the league signed, ratified, and implemented, determined to get the world to embrace his Fourteen Points, and increasingly wary of the motives of European leaders, Wilson insisted the league be included as an integral part of the peace treaty. The European plan had been to hold two conferences, the first to draft the peace treaty with the central powers and then a second under calmer circumstances to discuss and ratify the league.[37] The president rejected this plan. He was concerned that once the Allies got what they wanted in the first conference, they would have no interest in the league.[38] At best it would add another international conference and become another "wishy washy" "talk-fest at the Hague," creating "fog overhead and bog underfoot" as the Hague conventions, in Wilson's opinion, had done.[39] International conferences were giant dinner parties for lawyers and professional obscurantists, where clear principles of right and wrong got bogged down in the selfish grasping of the powerful nations. Besides, the carnage upon the battlefields of Europe was clear evidence to the president that previous European patterns of diplomacy were flawed.

Wilson was also concerned that a punitive peace enforced upon Germany would make it unlikely that the Germans would support it. It was necessary that all civilized nations joined the league. The Germans would not want anything to do with an international organization and system that proposed a *peace* dictated to them by the victorious Allies. He submitted a resolution to the Peace Conference to create a committee to frame the constitution of the league and to make it part of the final treaty. Clemenceau was opposed to the merging of the two, but Britain and Italy supported the move.[40] With their support Wilson became chairman of the League of Nations committee.

The battle to keep the league in the treaty did not go away. As the great powers found the larger group of nations too unwieldy to work with, the conference broke into smaller groups. The smallest and most important of these groups was the "Council of Four," which included the heads of state of Britain, France, Italy, and the United States. An irony not lost on Clemenceau or subsequent historians is that the proponent of "open covenants openly arrived at" insisted on secret councils to arrive at those covenants. On March 25th, at an early meeting of the Council of Four, Clemenceau again tried to separate the league from the peace treaty. He argued that if the Germans were not in the league, and he was determined that they would not be, they could not sign a treaty that included a ratification of the league. Wilson argued that the league would enforce the peace which the Germans had to agree to and therefore they should have the chance to record their agreement to it. There would be "so many threads" of the league in the peace treaty that one "cannot dissect" the treaty from the league.[41] Wilson was determined that there be a league. Germany and

By now

all democratic nations would eventually be in that league. With the support of Britain and Italy, he again prevailed. Clemenceau retained his objection but went on to other business.[42] To the president, the principle of peace without victory could now only be accomplished by the adoption of the league on his terms. He was as unbending on this as if his proposals were Moses' tablets of stone.

Lansing observed that the other members of the Council of Four began to use Wilson's idealistic principles against him to get more material goals, like territory or mineral rights. The British, who were the most supportive of the league in general, gave their support with the assumption that it would not affect their naval superiority or limit their colonial claims. They then used this support to broker other deals in their national interest. Other leaders at the conference discovered that the league was the ultimate bargaining chip when dealing with the American president.

Having survived attempts to make the league a separate issue, Wilson now faced these other battles. The president met some of these occasions with defiance and others with compromise. When the Italian leader, Vittorio Orlando, and his delegation walked out of the conference demanding the cession of Austrian territory to Italy, Wilson also threatened to leave, firing off an address to the Italian people from his own typewriter. He pulled from his pocket the greatest weapon he knew, his father's weapon, the preacher's weapon, the messenger's weapon: persuasive words. Appealing to the good heart of the Italian people he delivered his sermon. "America is Italy's friend. . . . [America] trusts Italy, and in her trust believes that Italy will ask nothing of her that cannot be made unmistakably consistent with those sacred obligations. Interest is not now in question, but the rights of peoples, . . . and above all the right of the world to peace."[43] Italian public response was evidently negative.[44] Increasingly, national interest clashed with Wilson's dictated "sacred obligations" and the international popular support that he was counting upon to put pressure on the European leaders dissolved.[45]

On other issues Wilson was willing to compromise. With the conference at a seeming impasse over colonial claims, Smuts suggested a step between empire and independence. He proposed that the *mature* democracies tutor the emerging nations until they were able to handle full independence.[46] It was a proposal that fit with Wilson's paternalistic tendency to see the nonwhite peoples as being in need of instruction, as he had in Latin America. For those not ready to give up the colonial system, it appeared to hold the possibility of a continuation of the system under another name.[47] If they could find the right wording, so that it would seem to comply with the *spirit* of the American proposals, Wilson would accept substantial deviations from his stated aims. This compromise allowed Wilson's vision for the league to move forward. In the short run, however, the compromise was less than the full "free, open-minded, and absolutely impartial adjustment of all colonial claims" that the president had publicly promised.

Former president William Howard Taft had urged the president to get language in the treaty that protected the Monroe Doctrine. Wilson secured such language, but at the cost of further concessions.[48] Some of the compromises allowed uncomfortable or controversial questions to be deferred to the league for later consideration. While it might seem this indicated that these issues were unimportant enough to the president that he was willing to defer them to a "wishy washy talk-fest at the Hague," Wilson single mindedly interpreted all the action as progress. The very fact that they were willing to defer issues for the league and World Court confirmed to the president's mind that the great powers were supporting the league.[49]

Deferring complicated issues also protected Wilson from having to face potential flaws in his plan. He was most comfortable seeing issues in terms of right and wrong. His speeches highlighted this attitude. But he had no clear solution for when right met right, as it often did when claims of national self-determination clashed. National groups were not conveniently grouped together according to neat natural borders or easily identifiable *good* leaders they could be *taught* to elect. Deferring complex matters to the league allowed Wilson to believe he had kept his principles unsullied, while the European leaders believed they had deferred politically unpalatable concessions, perhaps indefinitely. Lansing grew sick at heart as the deal unfolded. Versailles was a departure from the previous history of Vienna and the Hague, and it seemed to Lansing to be an unrealistic and fatally flawed departure.[50]

The compromise for which Wilson was most vilified by both Germany and the political left was on the issue of war reparations. He agreed with the other members of the Council of Four that Germany would pay for *civilian* losses, including some military pensions for those families that had lost a bread winner in the war. These losses quickly began to expand to include greater and greater Allied claims. John Foster Dulles, nephew of Robert Lansing, future secretary of state, and a junior member of the American delegation, recounted a meeting on the subject of reparations in which the president was "continuously finding new meanings and the necessity of broad application of principles previously enunciated. . . ."[51] Dulles pointed out the logical problem these reparations would cause. Wilson replied that "he did not feel bound by considerations of logic."[52] Dulles softened the retelling of the exchange and the president's remarks. Another witness to the meeting recalled the haggard and weary president, responding with much more heat, snapping impatiently: "I don't give a damn for logic!"[53] House and Lansing's fears of the weakness of the president as a negotiator were being realized before their eyes. The president was weary of haggling about details. He had in his own mind a clear central set of goals. The details were wearing him down and getting in his way. It was not just logic that he did not "give a damn" about, but technicalities as well. The particulars, so important to the rest of the council, would work themselves out if he could just get the league ratified. That was his one goal. The league would fix the legal trivia once it was established. As the conference went on and the president grew more exhausted, his views hardened. He became increasingly inflexible and impatient about technicalities and procedures.

Though the president was not interested in the details, it would be wrong to characterize him as unaware of technicalities or unable to grasp complicated arguments. In the meetings, the president's grasp of detail and the clarity with which he was able to sum up complex conversations camouflaged the simplicity of his goals. He was able to enumerate the points of very complicated discussions without proposing specifics to add to the plan. He was not interested in particulars other than where they were necessary to hasten ratification of the general outline of the league. The tension between the rigidity of his simple goal to get the league ratified and the vagueness and lack of concern he showed over the other details of the treaty created different perceptions in those who observed him at Paris. Some saw him as imperious and rigid, while others spoke of him as vague and unsure of himself. This difference of perception depended on which issues were under consideration.

Clemenceau commented on the American president's idealistic inflexibility on the league, the Fourteen Points, and the attitude of divine mission he displayed: "The good Lord Himself required only ten points; Wilson has fourteen."[54] "I can get on with you," Clemenceau told House, "You are practical . . . but talking to Wilson is something like talking to Jesus Christ!"[55] Keynes saw a different side to this inflexibility: "But in fact the president had thought out nothing; when it came to practice his ideas were nebulous and incomplete. He had no plan, no scheme, no constructive ideas whatever for clothing with the flesh of life the commandments he had thundered from the White House. He could have preached a sermon on any of them or have addressed a stately prayer to the Almighty for their fulfillment; but he could not frame their concrete application to the actual state of Europe."[56] Significantly, both those who thought Wilson too rigid and those who thought him too vague portrayed him in biblical imagery. The one aspect of his personality about which there was little debate at this time was the religious quality of his sense of mission. His manner, his words, his personal conviction that he was God's messenger to the international order, all combined to evoke this imagery in those who observed him.

Avoiding details was not an accident or oversight for Wilson. His policy was deliberately vague in regard to many of the particulars of the overall treaty. He had told Congress that "The [U.S.] has no desire to interfere in European affairs or to act as arbiter in European territorial disputes."[57] Lansing confirmed that the president was willing to stay out of the details of European squabbles. So long as he could determine the larger principles by which they would operate, he was content to leave the minutiae to others. Keynes, who had hoped for more, considered this a fatal flaw in the president's personality.

> Now it was that what I have called his theological or Presbyterian temperament became dangerous. . . . Although compromises were now necessary he remained a man of principle and the Fourteen Points a contract absolutely binding upon him. . . . he would do nothing that was contrary to his great profession of faith. Thus without any abate-

ment of the verbal inspiration of the Fourteen Points, they became a document for gloss and interpretation . . . the intellectual apparatus of self deception, by which . . . the president's forefathers had persuaded themselves that the course they thought it necessary to take was consistent with every syllable of the Pentateuch.[58]

Keynes was correct in this observation of Wilson's attitude toward the Fourteen Points. So long as they were accepted they would be interpreted as a living, adaptable document, as scripture and United States Constitution had been in the president's tradition. The Fourteen Points would embody the spirit of the age. Like the scriptures, they would be interpreted by each generation, mixing its spirit with the principles of justice and right upon which the document was founded.

The league and the Fourteen Points must be agreed upon. To Wilson this was all that mattered. Details and legalistic logic be damned! Details would work themselves out in time. Lansing noted that the president seldom forced the United States position into the treaty.[59] He believed the president had no definite outline or details for a treaty other than the Fourteen Points and allowed none of his advisors to put a specific outline or particulars together.[60] The details of the Versailles settlement were largely authored by the British and French.[61] Lansing was unable to see why this was of no concern to Wilson. The secretary of state did not have the whole picture. Being outside the president's confidence his legal mind could only see the lack of specific legal detail as a failure on the president's part. Wilson, who despised the technicalities of law, saw it as a strength. The Europeans and their lawyers could haggle over the trivia. America would stand above the fray with the ideas of freedom and justice that would eventually transform those details. America was right, and right would win. As long as the spirit and central structure of the league was adopted, and the international *presbytery* of nations agreed upon this document, it would eventually bring justice to the world.

The pressure on Wilson at this point was extraordinary. All his providential hopes for the world, his whole divine mission in life, became reduced to this one scrap of paper. It became the focus, the convergence, of his convictions about the importance of the task over the organization and his high regard for the written word properly interpreted. His lifelong immersion in covenant theology and his cultural background in Presbyterian church life, coupled with his own personality and sense of mission, made this hope more intense. To Wilson the principles were clear and simple. They defined the ultimate form that detail would take. When Lansing commented that the president's ideals blinded him to the material aims of the Europeans, he failed to grasp that it was not blindness at all—he simply did not care. Wilson cared greatly about the ideals, but very little about material aims. The task, in this case his mission, was embodied in the ideals which he believed would eventually exert control over the details of the organization and the final form it would take in the material world.[62] That organization would then define the righteous settlement of all international claims. Wilson believed this "scrap of paper" embodied the principles of the divine purpose of history and offered fulfillment of the yearnings of the people of the world. Everything in his life up to this point hinged on agreement being given to this document.

Wilson's hopes were realized. The document was agreed upon by the Peace Conference. On June 28, 1919 the humiliated German delegation signed the treaty in the Hall of Mirrors at Versailles. The League of Nations was part of the agreement, as well a very battered version of Wilson's points, if not quite the original fourteen. For all that Wilson had failed to get, his single-mindedness on his principles had achieved remarkable success. He was certain that the treaty spelled out the first steps toward decolonization, a moderation of the claims of the victors, an agreement in principle to conduct international business in a new way. Most importantly, the League of Nations, now part of an agreement that included a World Court, would fix the flaws of the treaty with the help of the United States. His job was done. The Senate would have no choice but to see the divine logic of this treaty and would be honor-bound to ratify it. Should he have to, he was willing to force the Senate to see their duty.[63] He worked on his message to the Senate while traveling home on the *George Washington*, believing his work was nearly done.

"The only legitimate object of organization is efficiency,"[64] Wilson said early in his first term in office. This idea of organizational efficiency was the crux of the task versus organization antinomy. An organization was only as good as its ability to achieve its task. In Wilson's mind, Article Ten of the league treaty made the new organization efficient. It required all nations connected to the league to "respect and preserve as against external aggression the territorial integrity and existing political independence of all Members of the League."[65]

Wilson's failure to consult the Senate now became the fateful mistake in his negotiations. While focusing on the Europeans he had forgotten his home audience. It was over Article Ten that the Senate battle over the treaty began. To some members it appeared that the president was taking the United States in a direction that departed from its history. The league covenant seemed a direct repudiation of George Washington's caution about staying out of European alliances. Article Ten seemed to pledge the United States, in advance, to come to the assistance of any nation in distress, regardless of the causes of the dispute. Wilson considered these concerns slanderous nonsense made up by people ignorant of his principles or by enemies of world peace. The league would resolve disputes without war. Any war, therefore, would pit an aggressor against the world, represented by the league, and the American people would be eager to support the righteous cause of the world.

Like a perfect storm, like tributaries coming together during a flood, Wilson's political convictions, his theological view of the world, his sense of mission, and his failing health converged at this moment as he began his battle with the Senate over the treaty. During this struggle Wilson's physical condition deteriorated, causing him to further harden his position and become, if possible, even less amenable to compromise. His health exacerbated the vulnerability of the other aspects of his personality and political convictions.

Adding impetus to his conviction that it was God's will he prevail over all opponents was the president's previously developed and published conviction that the chief executive was supreme in negotiating treaties. The battle with the Senate, sparked in part by Article Ten, has been the focus of much debate. Historian Daniel Stid has written that the views Wilson expressed on the absolute control the president had over foreign policy set him up for his collision with the Senate.[66] But it was more than that. The fight followed a pattern that Wilson's public struggles had displayed all of his adult life. It harkened back to his father's willingness to lose his pastorate and seminary chair in order to keep from abandoning his principles by allowing seminary students to attend the local Presbyterian church rather than the seminary chapel on Sundays.

For thirty-two years Wilson's academic and political writings had spelled out the principle he was fighting with the Senate over: presidential prerogative in foreign policy. Wilson published *Congressional Government: A Study in American Politics* in 1885.[67] In this work he expressed his deep admiration for the British parliamentary system. Wilson felt that the parliamentary system was more efficeint and more democratic. *Congressional Government* and the later article "Cabinet Government," which was published in the *Atlantic* by its young editor, Henry Cabot Lodge, espoused a greater role for Congress at the expense of the executive. Wilson believed that the best president was one whose leadership emerged from the body of the congress as did the leadership of the British prime minister. This would ensure a higher quality of leadership and a leader with greater power, invested by the representatives of the people to lead the nation. It was a system which mirrored, in many ways, the Presbyterian system of church government that he was familiar with. The pastor of a church or moderator of the general assembly emerged from the body of his fellow elders by the common recognition by his peers of his extraordinary abilities.

Wilson wrote of the Senate that "The greatest consultative privilege of the Senate,—the greatest in dignity, at least, if not in effect upon the interests of the country,—is its right to a ruling voice in the ratification of treaties with foreign powers."[68] *But*, this was not an unnuanced privilege. He went on to argue that organic considerations "have made it impossible that there should be any real consultation between the President and the Senate. . . ."[69] Whenever Wilson spoke of things *organic*, or the spirit of an institution, that part that was *organic* or *spirit* took precedent in his thought. The Senate's power was *legal*. He likened its role to that of an auditor's: "I do not consult the auditor who scrutinizes my accounts when I submit to him my books, my vouchers and a written report of the business I have negotiated. I do not take his advice or seek his consent; I simply ask his endorsement or invite his condemnation."[70] He argued that since the President was not part of the process of the Senate in approving the treaty, he had no reason to consult the senators when making a treaty.

The Senate had only one duty: to accept or reject the finished product. Even if they had reservations as to the wisdom of the treaty the president might have the country "so pledged in the view of the world to certain courses of action, that the Senate [would hesitate to bring] the appearance of dishonor which would follow its refusal to ratify."[71] Thus a president could "morally" bind the Senate to a treaty, which it would then be honor-bound to ratify because the spokesman for the government had given his word.

Wilson had focused on what he believed were the weaknesses of the American system in *Congressional Government*. At this point in the development of his thought he was convinced that the American system would be better if the president were more like a prime minister. Twenty-three years later, when he published *Constitutional Government in the United States*, his views had evolved. He still believed that the president need not consult the Senate in treaty making. But he felt that the presidency as it existed in the Constitution was a strength, as the person in the office was able, under certain circumstances, to embody the spirit of the nation, the party, and the government in one man. A strong president could do this unencumbered by membership in a congressional body. A member of Congress, with its multiple local and regional constituencies, could not do this.[72]

By 1908 President Wilson had developed a more organic vision of national government. He saw that the presidency had grown with the nation and had become stronger as the interpretation of the Constitution had evolved. The Constitution was a living thing rather than an inflexible legal document. "It is accountable to Darwin, not to Newton. It is modified by its environment, necessitated by its tasks, shaped to its functions by the sheer pressure of life. . . . There can be no successful government without leadership."[73] The fluidity of the Constitution allowed the president as leader to stamp himself on the people's understanding of the document itself. "The Presidents who have not made themselves leaders" failed to live in the spirit of the Constitution. They did not alter it. They did not put the imprint of the spirit of the nation which they themselves embodied on the understanding of the document.[74] "The Constitution of the United States is not a mere lawyer's document: it is a vehicle of life, and its spirit is always the spirit of the age."[75]

This elevated view of the presidency fit well with Wilson's conviction about his own divine mission. This mission was well suited to the opinions he had expressed in *Constitutional Government* on the power of the president in foreign policy: "One of the greatest of the President's powers . . . [is] his control, which is very absolute, of the foreign relations of the nation." While acknowledging the need to have the Senate ratify treaties, he wrote that the president "may guide every step of diplomacy. And to guide diplomacy is to determine what treaties must be made. . . . He need disclose no step of the negotiation until it is complete, and when in any matter it is completed the government is virtually committed."[76] The president alone negotiated treaties. On March 20, 1918, months before the Armistice, Wilson complained to House about the "folly of these League to Enforce Peace butters-in."[77] He was determined to guard jealously the presidential prerogative of treaty negotiation against all other contenders, popular or congressional.

As the president left for France for his second and final round of negotiations, he warned those who would try to oppose the league: "I want to utter this solemn warning, not in the way of a threat; the forces of the world do not threaten, they operate. The great tides of the world do not give notice that they are going to rise and run; they rise in their majesty and overwhelming might, and those who stand in the way are overwhelmed."[78] He believed a treaty on his terms was inevitable. The tides of the world and the inevitable direction of history would overwhelm all opposition. Upon his return to the United States, he believed that opposition had been overcome in Paris. The tide had risen, the rest of the world had acknowledged it. The United States Senate would be bound to ratify this treaty which was so evidently providential.

Eleven years after the publication of *Constitutional Government*, Wilson, now in the office of president, returned from his triumphant trip to Europe with a treaty in hand. It is apparent from his attitude leading up to the presentation of the treaty to the Senate that he was convinced the reality of American politics would conform to his principles. At a press conference a little more than an hour before his speech to the Senate, one reporter commented that the Senate was operating on the assumption that it could make reservations by majority vote.

The president replied, "That is a very dangerous assumption."[79] When asked if the treaty could be ratified with reservations the president snapped about "hypothetical questions" and said simply, "The Senate is going to ratify the treaty."[80]

On July 10, 1919 he introduced the treaty to the Senate. His address pulled all the elements of his thought and sense of divine calling together.[81] America had entered the war on a different footing from every other belligerent. "We entered the war as the disinterested champions of right." The entrance of America meant "salvation" to the Allies.[82] He employed the language of spiritual warfare from the gospels and the Revelation of St. John. He compared the old system of international relations to the image of Satan from Revelation: "The monster that had resorted to arms must be put in chains that could not be broken."[83] The phrases *final war* and *only hope for mankind* were rife with eschatological meaning. To show the need for the treaty he used Jesus' parable about the demon-possessed man who, having replaced the demon with nothing, was seven times worse upon its return.[84] "Again and again had the demon of war been cast out of the house of the peoples and the house swept clean by a treaty of peace; only to create a time when he would enter in again with spirits worse than himself." He explicitly gave the Treaty of Versailles the role in the current international order that his Christian theology gave to the Holy Spirit in the parable, or to Christ in the heart of the individual. The league was the "strong man" who could hold the house against the demon of war. To fail to ratify the treaty would "break the heart of the world."[85]

The president characterized himself as the embodiment of the spirit of a God-called nation carrying a divine message of redemption to the world. He was bringing a new and better covenant. "The stage is set, the destiny is disclosed. It has come about by no plan of our conceiving, but by the hand of God who has led us into this way. We cannot turn back. We can only go forward, with lifted eyes and freshened spirit, to follow the vision. It was of this that we dreamed at our birth. America shall in truth show the way. The light streams upon the path ahead, and nowhere else."[86] All the elements of his Calvinism, his idea of the United States as the "Redeemer Nation," his views as to how the political structures in America worked, and his own sense that he was at the pinnacle of fulfilling his divine mission intersected in this closing statement. The speech again harkened back to the language of "Christ's Army," written in his youth and returned to so often. He was the general leading Christ's army with the uplifted "sword of the spirit" as he addressed the Senate and nation. He could not fail. He did not even consider the possibility of failure. The obstacles had been overcome, the pharaohs confronted, the wilderness crossed, the promised land was in view.

Sadly for Wilson, politics is an antinomy of a completely different kind. Throughout the rest of July and August he battled his opponents in the Senate. They did not view their role as that of a mere auditor. Wilson reciprocated with a familiar obstinance. As he had done when his opponents tried to outmaneuver him at Princeton, as he had done when the *Lusitania* was torpedoed, as he had done upon his arrival in Paris, Wilson became inflexible in the face of external pressure. His relationship with his experienced friend and negotiator House, already distant, ceased altogether. The president no longer even bothered to open his former friend's letters. House had been too quick to attempt compromise with the Europeans, he had suggested the unfortunate March dinner with the Senate Foreign Relations Committee, he could not be trusted in negotiation with the Senate.[87] "Your dinner with the Senate Foreign Relations Committee was a failure as far as getting together was concerned," he told House bitterly.[88] Lansing, who also counseled negotiation or compromise, was disregarded and eventually dismissed.

Providence had provided a way out of other impasses. The president felt himself so clearly right on this issue, with such spiritual and legal authority on his side, that it was not possible he could fail. God would not let him fail after all he had come through to get to this place. Doubt was met with confident assertions that God and the people would force the Senate to come around. Paradise had the serpent; Wilson had Lodge and the Senate reservationists. The president was not tempted to taste the fruit of their reservations. To believe that God would let the treaty fail was unthinkable. It would imply that Satan had thwarted God's will.

In interviews with senators and the press, the president stated repeatedly that he was opposed to any reservations to the treaty. Occasionally he would leave the impression that he was willing to consider minor points of interpretation, but he never gave the slightest hint that he was willing to yield his presidential treaty-making role to anyone else. He had given his word. He had negotiated a treaty which may as well have been written on tablets of stone. The *spirit* of the treaty would fix the lawyer's language. Reasonable minds would make reasonable interpretations of the meaning of that language. With the help of the United States the international community would become reasonable. The hypothetical situations pointed to by his opponents would not occur. It was unreasonable to worry about such circumstances. Providence would not permit those conditions which might damage or destroy the new covenant of nations, this divinely ordained order.

Wilson argued his case using every real, potential, and imaginary crisis as evidence that the treaty needed to be ratified. He told reporters that "chaos might reign in Europe" if the Senate continued to delay ratification.[89] He blamed the rising cost of living on the failure of the Senate to ratify the treaty: "There can be no settled conditions here or elsewhere until the treaty of peace is out of the way and the work of liquidating the war has become the chief concern of our government and of the other governments of the world. . . . There can be no peace prices so long as our whole financial and economic system is on a war basis."[90] Everything was makeshift and provisional until the peace treaty was ratified.

In the meantime, Lodge and his Senate allies were stiffening their resistance. Having originally proposed that the reservations should be merely an expression of the Senate's concern, standing separate from the treaty, Senate leaders announced in the press on August 2, 1919, that the "reservations and understandings enumerated shall become a part of the treaty and shall not stand simply as a detached interpretation of the Senate."[91] The forces in favor of reservations were gaining strength. Some opposed the treaty under any circumstances, others claimed they were not opposing the treaty but simply wanted to make mild reservations, and others who supported the treaty were willing to concede some reservations in order to get some form of the treaty ratified.[92]

Wilson would have none of this. American sovereignty was not at stake, as those obsessed with Article Ten implied, but American

honor was. His personal honor and that of the presidential office was
at stake. The Senate could reject the treaty if it foolishly chose to, but
it could not change the word of the president already given. In a meeting with Gilbert Hitchcock, the Senate minority leader and an early
supporter of the league, he compared the treaty to the law of God.
He used Christ's words about the law of Moses: "We've got to remove
absolutely any possibility of the dotting of an 'i' or the crossing of
a 't'."[93] On July 18th, Wilson informed Wiseman privately that he
might have to concede some small reservation defining or interpreting
the language of the treaty.[94] But he went on to say that he "was setting
his face against any amendments or reservations."[95]

Soon even these small concessions disappeared from his language.
As he had in the past, Wilson grew increasingly inflexible in his position as the battle progressed. He saw only two camps: absolutely loyal,
unquestioning friends or evil foes. He was soon viewing the Senate
reservationists as foes no matter how mild the reservations. The *people*
were supporting him, he told Wiseman. He was after all, the embodiment of their collective spirit. Elected by them and by God for this
mission, he was already looking forward to his speaking tour when
he could rally their support in his mission.[96] The cheering mobs in
France were still in his mind.

On August 19, 1919, Wilson made one more attempt to meet
with the Senate Foreign Relations Committee to answer their questions about the treaty. It did not go well. The president was by this
time deeply entrenched and was only willing to inform the senators,
yet again, of his position. He would not discuss any potential reservations. The questions went quickly to the issue of Article Ten. He
stated that he saw the clauses of the treaty not as legal obligations but
as *moral* ones. The senators challenged the president as to what he had
meant by previous statements that the United States was *bound* by
some aspects of the treaty. He replied that he "did not use the word
'bound', but 'morally bound.'"[97] To Wilson this was a clear distinction between how he saw the treaty and how the reservationist senators were viewing it. In fact he had not used the term *morally bound* in
the document the senator cited but *bound*.[98]

This rewording of the facts and revisionist memory of his own
words added to the distrust of those in the Senate, particularly Lodge,

who already considered him dishonest. The rest of the meeting was an argument over the difference between *legal* and *moral* obligations.[99] Republican Senator Warren G. Harding of Ohio asked: "If there is nothing more than a moral obligation on the part of any member of the League, [then what use are] articles 10 and 11?"[100] The president's response reflected his own internal Presbyterian pattern of logic. A legal obligation, for the president, removed the antinomy of concurrently balancing differing principles. Moral obligations, on the other hand, answered all the objections raised by the reservationists about U.S. sovereignty. "When I speak of a legal obligation, I mean one that specifically binds you to do a particular thing under certain sanctions. Now a moral obligation is of course superior to a legal obligation, and, if I may say so, has a greater binding force; only there always remains in the moral obligation the right to exercise one's own judgment as to whether it is indeed incumbent . . . to do that thing. In every moral obligation there is an element of judgment. In a legal obligation there is not."[101]

This carefully phrased distinction went to the heart of the president's Presbyterian theology as it applied to the treaty. The law was fixed and unchanging, but *moral law* required the application of an inner moral judgment. It was a law of the spirit and thus one could follow the *spirit of the law*, not the letter, and still be obedient to the law itself. The president had taken these views and applied them to the Constitution. He had applied them to international law of blockade and neutrality. He had applied them to intervention in Mexico and Russia. Now he applied them to the Treaty of Versailles. The key was knowing the right thing to do, the will of providence. Righteous leaders would be able to look at the text of the law and use their judgment to locate an interpretation in line with the *spirit* of the intention. In the words of the Bible, they could "rightly divide the word of truth."[102]

The Senate was not convinced. The president's testimony, uncompromising in tone and filled with inaccuracies, hurt his cause among wavering senators. He therefore took his case to the people. Early in the morning of September 3, 1919, the presidential train pulled out of Washington, D.C., on a whirlwind tour of the nation. The president stopped in Columbus, Indianapolis, St. Louis, Kansas City,

St. Paul, Bismarck, Billings, Spokane, Tacoma, Seattle, Portland, San Francisco, Reno, Salt Lake City, Denver, and Pueblo. In all he traveled to over thirty-two cities in twenty-two days, with even more events and unscheduled stops in between.[103]

Wilson's speeches reiterated the divine nature of the treaty at every opportunity. He compared the treaty to the covenant of the seventeenth-century Scottish covenanters: "My ancestors were troublesome Scotchmen, and among them were some of that famous group that were known as the Covenanters. Very well, here is the Covenant of the League of Nations. I am a Covenanter!"[104] He emphasized that his covenant, the covenant of the league, was one of conscience, not of law. "It is absolutely left to the conscience of this nation. . . ."[105] The speeches grew more emotional and contradictory as the president pressed himself beyond the limits of his physical and emotional health. In one speech, in an early hint of his impending total collapse, he revised his ancestry and, to Lodge's horror, declared: "I have been bred, and am proud to have been bred, in the old Revolutionary stock which set this government up."[106] The *New York Herald* was quick to refute this claim: "Just what led President Wilson to claim Pilgrim forebears is not clear."[107]

In Pueblo, Colorado, in what would prove to be his last substantial public speech, he closed by mixing the language and syntax of the Psalms and the epistles of Paul and the Gospel of John with his own words, addressing the mission of America, the purpose of the treaty, and his own divine mission. "Now the mists of this great question have cleared away, I believe that men will see the truth, eye to eye and face to face. There is one thing that the American people always rise to and extend their hand to, and that is the truth of justice and of liberty and of peace. We have accepted that truth, and we are going to be led by it, and it is going to lead us, and, through us, the world, out into pastures of quietness and peace such as the world never dreamed of before."[108]

Pueblo was his last speech. At two o'clock the next morning, September 26th, Grayson was summoned to the president's car. Wilson had been overcome by a complete physical and mental collapse. Grayson found him in pain, highly agitated, his face twitching uncontrollably and unable to breath.[109] Edith and Grayson worked with him for the next two hours. His speech was unintelligible, his left side partially paralyzed. He was unable to control his tears.[110] The rest of the speaking tour was called off and the president was rushed back to Washington. Six days later, on October 2nd, he suffered a massive stroke and was subsequently bed-ridden, unable to communicate or walk.[111]

Though Wilson continued the fight for ratification of the treaty—from his bed after he had recovered somewhat, and later from a wheel chair in the oval office, the fight was for all practical purposes over. The president's mind was affected by the stroke. His wife and doctor kept him away from much information that could have helped him make decisions if he had been able or so inclined.[112] For weeks and perhaps months the administration carried on through inertia, with Edith and Grayson making the few decisions that could not be postponed with varying input from the president.

Despite the stroke, Wilson retained his providential sense of mission. He continued to believe, against all evidence to the contrary, that the League of Nations covenant would prevail and that the Treaty of Versailles would pass the Senate without reservation. On November 19, 1919, seven weeks after his stroke, the treaty was defeated in the first of three Senate votes. On March 19, 1920 it was defeated in the second vote. Though flexibility on some mild reservations as to interpretation would likely have enabled the treaty to pass in some form, Wilson would have nothing to do with compromise. By this point he was incapable of any deviation from what he now considered a divine document.

Depressed and unable to sleep following the second defeat of the treaty, he asked Grayson to come to his bedside and read the scripture to him. He had the doctor turn to a passage that summed up his internal resolve in the face of all external evidence. "We are troubled on every side, yet not distressed; we are perplexed, but not in despair; persecuted, but not forsaken; cast down, but not destroyed."[113] "The Devil is a busy man," he told Grayson.[114] He then expressed the same sense of providence which had pressed him this far: "If I were not a Christian, I think I should go mad, but my faith in God holds me to the belief that He is in some way working out his own plans through human perversities and mistakes."[115] He continued to see the treaty fight as a battle between good and evil, a contest in which the truth he

held internally was destined to triumph over all uncomfortable facts
to the contrary. His inner faith would triumph over troubling reality;
the divine antinomy was at work in the affairs of men. God understood even if men did not.

The November 1920 elections put Harding in the White House,
on a platform that promised consideration of a League of Nations
but which rejected the Wilsonian version of the league. Democrat
James Cox, who had promised to support the existing covenant and
who Wilson was confident would win, was defeated in a landslide.
The people, in whose name Wilson had crusaded, clearly preferred
Harding's "return to normalcy" to further crusades for a righteous
world. Wilson continued to make feeble attempts to get the league
reconsidered. He fumed at the disarray in Europe, believing the Europeans only lacked American participation to make the league work.
He took no personal responsibility, however, for failures at Versailles
or United States failure to join the league. In late 1923, to the horror
of those close to him who knew his condition, he began considering a
run for president in the 1924 elections.[116] In the years following defeat
of the treaty his internal antinomy had again reprocessed the facts to
fit his preconceived belief in its ultimate triumph. "I would rather
fail in a cause that some day will triumph than win in a cause that I
know some day will fail."[117] As with Ellen's death, he began to see in
this failure the hand of God. His past failures had been only apparent
and temporary, each following a hard fought battle, each resulting in
an even greater victory. Failure at law had led to a successful academic
career. Failure to get his policies adopted at Princeton had led to the
governorship of New Jersey and to the presidency. Failure to get the
league ratified must lead to something better.

"I think it was best after all that the United States did not join the
League of Nations," he told his daughter Margaret. "[O]ur entrance
into the league at the time I returned from Europe might have been
only a personal victory." Because it would have been *personal*, it would
have been tainted, flawed, selfish. God had reined him in personally,
but that was not a failure, merely a delay. The purposes of God would
be fully realized. "Now when the American people join the league it
will be because they are convinced it is the only right time for them
to do it. Perhaps God knew better than I did after all."[118] Wilson

reprocessed the facts to fit his view of the providence of God. As long as he remained alive he continued to believe he had a divine plan to accomplish. He was still speaking of "peace without victory" as late as December 1923.[119] He continued to battle the Senate from his house on S Street, still asserting the president's absolute right in foreign policy, still interpreting the Senate's constitutionally defined treaty powers through his own internal antinomy. He remarked to a reporter in his last interview only a few months before his death: "Outside the United States, the Senate does not amount to a damn; and inside the United States the Senate is mostly despised; they haven't had a thought down there in fifty years."[120] The Senate as an organization had failed in its task. They were all, Democrats and Republicans alike, "damned."

On Wilson's last Armistice Day, November 11, 1923, a crowd gathered outside the house on S Street. Looking weak and old, the former president was helped onto the steps, where he stood to greet the crowd and make his final public address. Breaking down with emotion repeatedly, he spoke to the crowd in the same confident words that he had always used, though in a much weaker voice, about the triumph of the mission that he believed God had called him to accomplish. In the language of his Presbyterian father, he closed his speech with an expression of his continued determination that providence would yet vindicate him. "I am not one of those that have the least anxiety about the triumph of the principles I have stood for. I have seen fools resist Providence before and I have seen the destruction, as will come upon these again—utter destruction and contempt. That we shall prevail is as sure as that God reigns."[121] At 11:15 a.m. on February 3, 1924, Woodrow Wilson died at his home on S Street.

Republican president Herbert Hoover, who served as head of the famine relief program in war-torn Europe, said that Wilson's presidency "was a Greek tragedy, not on the stage of the imagination, but the lives of nations."[122] Wilson's "tragedy," however, had more to do with Jerusalem than Athens. It was a tragedy of faith. Arthur Link rightly observed that Wilson had an "absolute conviction that God had ordered the universe from the beginning, the faith that God used men for his own purposes." From this came his "sure sense of destiny and a feeling of intimate connection with the sources of power. . . .

Faith in God and submission to the Christian ethic underlay most of Wilson's political assumptions and fired his ambition to serve the Almighty by serving his fellow men."[123] In the end Wilson's faith in providence became inextricably entwined with his own inner voice. Faith inspired the best and the worst of Woodrow Wilson, his rise and his fall. It caused him to imagine a better, more just, more noble world, a vision that inspired the loyalty of those who followed him. It also caused him to deceive himself into believing that his personal quest for political power was a selfless act of obedience to providence. The threads of Wilson's faith are the brightest and the darkest antinomies in the tapestry that was his life.

Epilogue

So what might we conclude about the issue of American foreign policy and faith? When looking at the record of individual presidents, evidence of personal faith or the resulting worldview produced by that faith is overshadowed by very real temporal issues, which overwhelm their policies with an avalanche of competing concerns. Trying to coax out the threads of extrarational influences, such as faith, is a challenge. The difficulty proposed in the introduction of this book, that of studying the extrarational actions of people from a rational point of view, is very real. Yet for the majority of the world throughout history, religion has been deeply entwined with politics and foreign policy. As much as historians would like for the rational to fully explain this history, it simply does not. The enlightenment approach to history is flawed in that it is incomplete. People continue to be more than rational and make decisions on more than reason. They continue to find it necessary to believe.

Following the 2001 attacks on the World Trade Center in New York there was an increased interest in the role of religion in the world. This newly discovered role prompted numerous books, articles, documentaries, and news reports. Many of these were produced to examine extremist religion in politics. This is of particular interest during the administration of George W. Bush with its specific character, but had larger implications on the study of American international policy. It is tempting to make comparisons between the evangelistic zeal of the Wilson administration in its attempt to remake the world at the beginning of the twentieth century and the neoconservative vision

of the second President Bush at the beginning of the twenty-first
century. That temptation should be resisted. It is a different world, a
different theological framework, and the United States is a different
nation. Where the similarity does hold, however, is that both presidents viewed the world through the template of faith.

Religious faith is often a softer albeit more pervasive, undercurrent in an individual politician's political life than the extremes that
get attention. In 2007, during the run-up to the 2008 elections, the
Democratic candidates for president went out of their way to assure
American voters of their faith.[1] This attempted to mirror the success
that Republicans had made in the previous three decades assuring voters of their own religious faith. What this demonstrated is that in
American politics faith is reasonable. It is also reasonable to examine
the way that faith influences the rational political decisions of policy
makers. In time the religious history of American presidents and their
foreign policy should be written. It would contribute a greatly needed
piece to the understanding of international history.

But how shall we conclude the story of faith and Woodrow Wilson? Are there *lessons* to be learned? Despite Warren Harding's "return
to normalcy" and the general desire of the American public to aban-
don idealistic international causes, Wilson continued to believe that
his policies would prevail. The evidence suggests he died believing.
This pattern of trust in the final triumph of truth as he saw it, contra
evidence, is well documented. It was an unshakable hope because it
was based upon faith rather than reason. Historian Richard Gamble
brought a thoughtful contribution to the discourse of foreign relations history in his book *The War for Righteousness*.[2] He finds this kind
of faith, the kind held by the liberal reformers during the Progressive
Era, fatally flawed.

American theologian Reinhold Niebuhr might have agreed with
Gamble. Niebuhr, disillusioned by the presumption of his own age,
described America following the presidency of Woodrow Wilson, the
president who most disappointed him, as a nation in its infancy. America had to grow up, to get beyond its fascination with righteousness.
For Niebuhr this infantile presumption should have been dealt with
by two world wars. In his "Irony of American History," he despairs of
any "War for Righteousness." This cold and sinful age can only pro-

duce greater and lesser sins and the best we can do is to promote the cause of lesser sins. Niebuhr's religion seemed cold to some, though he would call it *realistic*. Niebuhr's church kept its parishioners from disillusionment. But America did not come to Niebuhr's revival. As a mature superpower the United States ought to have learned from the tragic consequences of the Marne, Ypres, Versailles, and Nuremberg. By the beginning of the twenty-first century it still has not. In this new realistic narrative the neoconservatives are playing Peter Pan with a Woodrow Wilson-styled foreign policy. But, is not this the irony of all history? Faith is an integral part of humanity. If not a religious then a secular faith—neither Hitler nor Stalin fit the traditional view of religious faith, yet extrarational approaches to policy can be cited in a study of either leader. There are the unmistakable patterns of faith, though not faith in God or divine providence. So perhaps it is not faith rather than reason which matters. If both faith and reason are to be present, then what matters is what kind of faith and what kind of reason.

The historic record shows that we as human beings cannot safely promote idealism in youth or a nation without the dangers of idealistic excess. The longing for a good or better world leads to a sense of mission, but mission can lead to presumption. Those who hope for a better world can, if given the power, also do great harm. This is a fact of human existence. By recognizing and recording human weakness, flaw, and error, however, and writing honest histories about them, we may be able to help those who read history to avoid making similar mistakes. Even if this is not possible, we must recognize that faith exists and must be accounted for. It has been and will remain a powerful force in human experience and in history.

Woodrow Wilson's last Armistice Day need not be where hope for a better world will always end. The broken Wilson in his final months may warn us of the absurdity of hope, but he also speaks to us of its power. Even the disillusioned Niebuhr recognized that humans could not exist without that hope. In "The Irony of American History" he wrote: "Nothing worth doing can be achieved in our lifetime, therefore we must be saved by hope."[3] Having escaped the sins of presumption and despair, how do we as historians, or more importantly as a people and a nation, keep ourselves from falling into the existential hell of crude fatalism? It would seem that we may do this by accepting the fact that faith, hope, and love remain a part of human experience. No matter how reasonable we become there are simply moments when the mind will make reasonable what the heart has determined. Perhaps the best that we can hope for is that the determination which springs from this faith will be mixed with humility.

Appendix I

"Christ's Army"
A Religious Essay by Woodrow Wilson
August 17, 1876

One of the favorite figures with sacred writers in their references to the inhabitants of this world is that of representing mankind as divided into two great armies. The field of battle is the world. From the abodes of righteousness advances the host of God's people under the leadership of Christ. Immediately behind the great Captain of Salvation come the veteran regiments of the soldiers of the cross with steady tread, their feet shod with the preparation of the Gospel of Peace, girt about with truth, their breastplates of righteousness glittering beneath the bright rays of their Master's love, each one grasping the sword of the Spirit. Later come the younger troops all eager for the fray. From the opposite side of the field, advancing from the tents of wickedness, come the hosts of sin led by the Prince of Lies himself, riding upon death's horse. Behind him a mighty army marshalled by fiends under the dark banners of iniquity. The object of the warfare on the part of the first is to gain glory for their Great Leader as well as the best good of the conquered by persuading them to leave the ranks of the evil one and enlist under their great Redeemer; that of the other to entice as many as will listen to them to go with them by the alluring paths of worldliness to everlasting destruction. The foes meet upon the great battle field of every-day life. With one sweeping charge the Christian band falls upon the overwhelming numbers of the Prince of Darkness and are met with a cloud of fiery darts from the hands of the Evil One. The battle waxes fierce. Some of the Christian leaders faithfully and eagerly press onward, rallying their broken ranks more vigorously upon every repulse. Others stand with folded arms,

only now and then languidly issuing an order or encouraging their
followers, and ever incurring the displeasure of their gracious Master
by failing to carry out his orders or properly marshall and encourage
his forces. The followers of the former, fight manfully, with only here
and there a laggard or coward; those of the latter partake of the spirit
of their leaders and do little towards gaining the battle. The hosts of
sin, ever and anon charging, break through the weak portions of the
opposing battalions, and then again quail before the uplifted swords
of the Spirit. Here, the plumes streaming from the glistening helmets
of salvation are seen among the retreating brigades of sin; there, Satan
leads his followers to victory over the dead bodies of many a soldier of
the Cross. Thus the battle of life progresses and the army of Saints ever
gains ground under divine generalship; now slowly, now rapidly, driving before them with irresistible force the broken ranks of the enemy.

Surely in this great contest there is a part for every one, and each
one will be made to render a strict account of his conduct on the
day of battle. Will any one hesitate as to the part he shall take in this
conflict? Will any one dare to enlist under the banners of the Prince
of Lies, under who dark folds he only marches to the darkness of hell?
For there is no middle course, no neutrality. Each and every one must
enlist either with the followers of Christ or those of Satan. How much
more glorious to fight for the divine Prince of Peace, under whose glorious standards, whose shining folds are inscribed with *Love to God*, he
will advance to sure victory and an everlasting reward! All professing
Christians are, no doubt, more or less enthused by such thoughts as
these, and hope that they can feel themselves soldiers in Christ's great
army; but they do not *know* that they are such. Why should they not
know? If they would be assured of the fact that their names are in the
great Roll Book, let them fight for Christ. Ah! but how do this? As
you would fight for any other cause. You know your enemies. They
are evil thoughts, evil desires, evil associations. To avoid evil thoughts
altogether is, of course, impossible. But whenever one of these subtle
warriors of evil attacks you, do not fear to test your breastplate; wield
with power the sword of the Spirit and with skill the shield of faith.
Overcome evil desires, those powerful and ever present enemies, by
constant watchfulness and with the strong weapon of prayer, and by
cultivating those heavenly desires which are sure to root out the evil

one. Avoid evil associations, evil companions. No one can make a good soldier who keeps company with the emissaries and friends of the enemy. These companions can be avoided by avoiding the places where they are to be found and seeking the more congenial and pleasant company of the good and upright, whose companionship will strengthen you in the struggle by making you feel that you are not alone in it. In every minor thing watch yourself and let no fiery dart enter your soul. One who thus faithfully does his duty and purifies himself in the smallest things has little to fear from the foe, and, if he withal leads others by his example and precept to do likewise, and fears not to warn the enemies of the Cross to turn from the error of their ways, he may rest assured that his name is enrolled among the soldiers of the Cross. Twiwood.*

Printed in the Wilmington North Carolina Presbyterian, August 23, 1876

* Twiwood was Wilson's pen name in this series of articles.

Appendix II

Wilson's "Fourteen Points" Address to Congress

Gentlemen of the Congress . . .

It will be our wish and purpose that the processes of peace, when they are begun, shall be absolutely open and that they shall involve and permit henceforth no secret understandings of any kind. The day of conquest and aggrandizement is gone by; so is also the day of secret covenants entered into in the interest of particular governments and likely at some unlooked-for moment to upset the peace of the world. It is this happy fact, now clear to the view of every public man whose thoughts do not still linger in an age that is dead and gone, which makes it possible for every nation whose purposes are consistent with justice and the peace of the world to avow now or at any other time the objects it has in view.

We entered this war because violations of right had occurred which touched us to the quick and made the life of our own people impossible unless they were corrected and the world secured once for all against their recurrence. What we demand in this war, therefore, is nothing peculiar to ourselves. It is that the world be made fit and safe to live in; and particularly that it be made safe for every peace-loving nation which, like our own, wishes to live its own life, determine its own institutions, be assured of justice and fair dealing by the other peoples of the world as against force and selfish aggression. All the peoples of the world are in effect partners in this interest, and for our own part we see very clearly that unless justice be done to others it will not be done to us. The program of the world's peace, therefore, is our program; and that program, the only possible program, as we see it, is this:

I.   Open covenants of peace, openly arrived at, after which there shall be no private international understandings of any kind but diplomacy shall proceed always frankly and in the public view.

II.   Absolute freedom of navigation upon the seas, outside territorial waters, alike in peace and in war, except as the seas may be closed in whole or in part by international action for the enforcement of international covenants.

III. The removal, so far as possible, of all economic barriers and the establishment of an equality of trade conditions among all the nations consenting to the peace and associating themselves for its maintenance.

IV.   Adequate guarantees given and taken that national armaments will be reduced to the lowest point consistent with domestic safety.

V.   A free, open-minded, and absolutely impartial adjustment of all colonial claims, based upon a strict observance of the principle that in determining all such questions of sovereignty the interests of the populations concerned must have equal weight with the equitable claims of the government whose title is to be determined.

VI.   The evacuation of all Russian territory and such a settlement of all questions affecting Russia as will secure the best and freest cooperation of the other nations of the world in obtaining for her an unhampered and unembarrassed opportunity for the independent determination of her own political development and national policy and assure her of a sincere welcome into the society of free nations under institutions of her own choosing; and, more than a welcome, assistance also of every kind that she may need and may herself desire. The treatment accorded Russia by her sister nations in the months to come will be the acid test of their good will, of their comprehension of her needs as distinguished from their own interests, and of their intelligent and unselfish sympathy.

VII. Belgium, the whole world will agree, must be evacuated and restored, without any attempt to limit the sovereignty which she enjoys in common with all other free nations. No other single act will serve as this will serve to restore confidence among the nations in the laws which they have themselves set and determined for the government of their relations with one another. Without this healing act the whole structure and validity of international law is forever impaired.

VIII. All French territory should be freed and the invaded portions restored, and the wrong done to France by Prussia in 1871 in the matter of Alsace-Lorraine, which has unsettled the peace of the world for nearly fifty years, should be righted, in order that peace may once more be made secure in the interest of all.

IX. A readjustment of the frontiers of Italy should be effected along clearly recognizable lines of nationality.

X. The peoples of Austria-Hungary, whose place among the nations we wish to see safeguarded and assured, should be accorded the freest opportunity of autonomous development.

XI. Rumania, Serbia, and Montenegro should be evacuated; occupied territories restored; Serbia accorded free and secure access to the sea; and the relations of the several Balkan states to one another determined by friendly counsel along historically established lines of allegiance and nationality; and international guarantees of the political and economic independence and territorial integrity of the several Balkan states should be entered into.

XII. The Turkish portions of the present Ottoman Empire should be assured a secure sovereignty, but the other nationalities which are now under Turkish rule should be assured an undoubted security of life and an absolutely unmolested opportunity of an autonomous development, and the Dardanelles should be permanently opened as a free passage to the ships and commerce of all nations under international guarantees.

XIII. An independent Polish state should be erected which should include the territories inhabited by indisputably Polish populations, which should be assured a free and secure access to the sea, and whose political and economic independence and territorial integrity should be guaranteed by international covenant.

XIV. A general association of nations must be formed under specific covenants for the purpose of affording mutual guarantees of political independence and territorial integrity to great and small states alike.

In regard to these essential rectifications of wrong and assertions of right we feel ourselves to be intimate partners of all the governments and peoples associated together against the Imperialists. We cannot be separated in interest or divided in purpose. We stand together until the end.

For such arrangements and covenants we are willing to fight and to continue to fight until they are achieved; but only because we wish the right to prevail and desire a just and stable peace such as can be secured only by removing the chief provocations to war, which this program does not remove. We have no jealousy of German greatness, and there is nothing in this program that impairs it. We grudge her no achievement or distinction of learning or of pacific enterprise such as have made her record very bright and very enviable. We do not wish to injure her or to block in any way her legitimate influence or power. We do not wish to fight her either with arms or with hostile arrangements of trade if she is willing to associate herself with us and the other peace-loving nations of the world in covenants of justice and law and fair dealing. We wish her only to accept a place of equality among the peoples of the world,—the new world in which we now live,—instead of a place of mastery.

Neither do we presume to suggest to her any alteration or modification of her institutions. But it is necessary, we must frankly say, and necessary as a preliminary to any intelligent dealings with her on our part, that we should know whom her spokesmen speak for when they speak to us, whether for the Reichstag majority or for the military party and the men whose creed is imperial domination.

We have spoken now, surely, in terms too concrete to admit of any further doubt or question. An evident principle runs through the whole program I have outlined. It is the principle of justice to all peoples and nationalities, and their right to live on equal terms of liberty and safety with one another, whether they be strong or weak. Unless this principle be made its foundation no part of the structure of international justice can stand. The people of the United States could act upon no other principle; and to the vindication of this principle they are ready to devote their lives, their honor, and everything that they possess. The moral climax of this the culminating and final war for human liberty has come, and they are ready to put their own strength, their own highest purpose, their own integrity and devotion to the test.

Appendix III

The Covenant of the League of Nations

THE HIGH CONTRACTING PARTIES, In order to promote international co-operation and to achieve international peace and security by the acceptance of obligations not to resort to war by the prescription of open, just and honourable relations between nations by the firm establishment of the understandings of international law as the actual rule of conduct among Governments, and by the maintenance of justice and a scrupulous respect for all treaty obligations in the dealings of organised peoples with one another Agree to this Covenant of the League of Nations.

ARTICLE 1.

The original Members of the League of Nations shall be those of the Signatories which are named in the Annex to this Covenant and also such of those other States named in the Annex as shall accede without reservation to this Covenant. Such accession shall be effected by a Declaration deposited with the Secretariat within two months of the coming into force of the Covenant Notice thereof shall be sent to all other Members of the League. Any fully self-governing State, Dominion, or Colony not named in the Annex may become a Member of the League if its admission is agreed to by two-thirds of the Assembly provided that it shall give effective guarantees of its sincere intention to observe its international obligations, and shall accept such regulations as may be prescribed by the League in regard to its military, naval, and air forces and armaments. Any Member of the League may, after two

years' notice of its intention so to do, withdraw from the League, provided that all its international obligations and all its obligations under
this Covenant shall have been fulfilled at the time of its withdrawal.

ARTICLE 2.

The action of the League under this Covenant shall be effected through
the instrumentality of an Assembly and of a Council, with a permanent Secretariat.

ARTICLE 3.

The Assembly shall consist of Representatives of the Members of the
League. The Assembly shall meet at stated intervals and from time to
time as occasion may require at the Seat of the League or at such other
place as may be decided upon. The Assembly may deal at its meetings
with any matter within the sphere of action of the League or affecting
the peace of the world. At meetings of the Assembly each Member
of the League shall have one vote, and may not have more than three
Representatives.

ARTICLE 4.

The Council shall consist of Representatives of the Principal Allied
and Associated Powers, together with Representatives of four other
Members of the League. These four Members of the League shall be
selected by the Assembly from time to time in its discretion. Until
the appointment of the Representatives of the four Members of the
League first selected by the Assembly, Representatives of Belgium,
Brazil, Spain, and Greece shall be members of the Council. With the
approval of the majority of the Assembly, the Council may name additional Members of the League whose Representatives shall always be
members of the Council; the Council with like approval may increase
the number of Members of the League to be selected by the Assembly
for representation on the Council. The Council shall meet from time
to time as occasion may require, and at least once a year, at the Seat
of the League, or at such other place as may be decided upon. The

Council may deal at its meetings with any matter within the sphere of action of the League or affecting the peace of the world. Any Member of the League not represented on the Council shall be invited to send a Representative to sit as a member at any meeting of the Council during the consideration of matters specially affecting the interests of that Member of the League. At meetings of the Council, each Member of the League represented on the Council shall have one vote, and may have not more than one Representative.

ARTICLE 5.

Except where otherwise expressly provided in this Covenant or by the terms of the present Treaty, decisions at any meeting of the Assembly or of the Council shall require the agreement of all the Members of the League represented at the meeting. All matters of procedure at meetings of the Assembly or of the Council, including the appointment of Committees to investigate particular matters, shall be regulated by the Assembly or by the Council and may be decided by a majority of the Members of the League represented at the meeting. The first meeting of the Assembly and the first meeting of the Council shall be summoned by the President of the United States of America.

ARTICLE 6.

The permanent Secretariat shall be established at the Seat of the League. The Secretariat shall comprise a Secretary General and such secretaries and staff as may be required. The first Secretary General shall be the person named in the Annex; thereafter the Secretary General shall be appointed by the Council with the approval of the majority of the Assembly. The secretaries and staff of the Secretariat shall be appointed by the Secretary General with the approval of the Council. The Secretary General shall act in that capacity at all meetings of the Assembly and of the Council. The expenses of the Secretariat shall be borne by the Members of the League in accordance with the apportionment of the expenses of the International Bureau of the Universal Postal Union.

ARTICLE 7.

The Seat of the League is established at Geneva. The Council may at any time decide that the Seat of the League shall be established elsewhere. All positions under or in connection with the League, including the Secretariat, shall be open equally to men and women. Representatives of the Members of the League and officials of the League when engaged on the business of the League shall enjoy diplomatic privileges and immunities. The buildings and other property occupied by the League or its officials or by Representatives attending its meetings shall be inviolable.

ARTICLE 8.

The Members of the League recognise that the maintenance of peace requires the reduction of national armaments to the lowest point consistent with national safety and the enforcement by common action of international obligations. The Council, taking account of the geographical situation and circumstances of each State, shall formulate plans for such reduction for the consideration and action of the several Governments. Such plans shall be subject to reconsideration and revision at least every ten years. After these plans shall have been adopted by the several Governments, the limits of armaments therein fixed shall not be exceeded without the concurrence of the Council. The Members of the League agree that the manufacture by private enterprise of munitions and implements of war is open to grave objections. The Council shall advise how the evil effects attendant upon such manufacture can be prevented, due regard being had to the necessities of those Members of the League which are not able to manufacture the munitions and implements of war necessary for their safety. The Members of the League undertake to interchange full and frank information as to the scale of their armaments, their military, naval, and air programmes and the condition of such of their industries as are adaptable to war-like purposes.

ARTICLE 9.

A permanent Commission shall be constituted to advise the Council on the execution of the provisions of Articles 1 and 8 and on military, naval, and air questions generally.

ARTICLE 10.

The Members of the League undertake to respect and preserve as against external aggression the territorial integrity and existing political independence of all Members of the League. In case of any such aggression or in case of any threat or danger of such aggression the Council shall advise upon the means by which this obligation shall be fulfilled.

ARTICLE 11.

Any war or threat of war, whether immediately affecting any of the Members of the League or not, is hereby declared a matter of concern to the whole League, and the League shall take any action that may be deemed wise and effectual to safeguard the peace of nations. In case any such emergency should arise the Secretary General shall on the request of any Member of the League forthwith summon a meeting of the Council. It is also declared to be the friendly right of each Member of the League to bring to the attention of the Assembly or of the Council any circumstance whatever affecting international relations which threatens to disturb international peace or the good understanding between nations upon which peace depends.

ARTICLE 12.

The Members of the League agree that if there should arise between them any dispute likely to lead to a rupture, they will submit the matter either to arbitration or to inquiry by the Council, and they agree in no case to resort to war until three months after the award by the arbitrators or the report by the Council. In any case under this Article the award of the arbitrators shall be made within a reasonable time, and the report of the Council shall be made within six months after the submission of the dispute.

ARTICLE 13.

The Members of the League agree that whenever any dispute shall arise between them which they recognise to be suitable for submission to arbitration and which cannot be satisfactorily settled by diplomacy, they will submit the whole subject-matter to arbitration. Disputes as to the interpretation of a treaty, as to any question of international law, as to the existence of any fact which if established would constitute a breach of any international obligation, or as to the extent and nature of the reparation to be made or any such breach, are declared to be among those which are generally suitable for submission to arbitration. For the consideration of any such dispute the court of arbitration to which the case is referred shall be the Court agreed on by the parties to the dispute or stipulated in any convention existing between them. The Members of the League agree that they will carry out in full good faith any award that may be rendered, and that they will not resort to war against a Member of the League which complies therewith. In the event of any failure to carry out such an award, the Council shall propose what steps should be taken to give effect thereto.

ARTICLE 14.

The Council shall formulate and submit to the Members of the League for adoption plans for the establishment of a Permanent Court of International Justice. The Court shall be competent to hear and determine any dispute of an international character which the parties thereto submit to it. The Court may also give an advisory opinion upon any dispute or question referred to it by the Council or by the Assembly.

ARTICLE 15.

If there should arise between Members of the League any dispute likely to lead to a rupture, which is not submitted to arbitration in accordance with Article 13, the Members of the League agree that they will submit the matter to the Council. Any party to the dispute may effect such submission by giving notice of the existence of the dispute to the Secretary General, who will make all necessary arrangements for a full investigation and consideration thereof. For this purpose the parties to the dispute will communicate to the Secretary General, as promptly as possible, statements of their case with all the relevant facts and papers, and the Council may forthwith direct the publication thereof. The Council shall endeavour to effect a settlement of the dispute, and if such efforts are successful, a statement shall be made public giving such facts and explanations regarding the dispute and the terms of settlement thereof as the Council may deem appropriate. If the dispute is not thus settled, the Council either unanimously or by a majority vote shall make and publish a report containing a statement of the facts of the dispute and the recommendations which are deemed just and proper in regard thereto. Any Member of the League represented on the Council may make public a statement of the facts of the dispute and of its conclusions regarding the same. If a report by the Council is unanimously agreed to by the members thereof other than the Representatives of one or more of the parties to the dispute, the Members of the League agree that they will not go to war with any party to the dispute which complies with the recommendations of the report. If the Council fails to reach a report which is unanimously agreed to by the members thereof, other than the Representatives of one or more of the parties to the dispute, the Members of the League reserve to themselves the right to take such action as they shall consider necessary for the maintenance of right and justice. If the dispute between the parties is claimed by one of them, and is found by the Council, to arise out of a matter which by international law is solely within the domestic jurisdiction of that party, the Council shall so report, and shall make no recommendation as to its settlement. The Council may in any case under this Article refer the dispute to the Assembly. The dispute shall be so referred at the request of either party to the dispute, provided that such request be made within fourteen days after the submission of the dispute to the Council. In any case referred to the Assembly, all the provisions of this Article and of Article 12 relating to the action and powers of the Council shall apply to the action and powers of the Assembly, provided that a report made by the Assembly, if concurred in by the Representatives of those Members of the League represented on the Council and of a majority of the other Members of the League, exclusive in each case of the Representatives of the parties to the dispute shall have the same force as a report by the Council concurred in by all the members thereof other than the Representatives of one or more of the parties to the dispute.

ARTICLE 16.

Should any Member of the League resort to war in disregard of its covenants under Articles 12, 13, or 15, it shall ipso facto be deemed to have committed an act of war against all other Members of the League, which hereby undertake immediately to subject it to the severance of all trade or financial relations, the prohibition of all intercourse between their nations and the nationals of the covenant-breaking State, and the prevention of all financial, commercial, or personal intercourse between the nationals of the covenant-breaking State and the nationals of any other State, whether a Member of the League or not. It shall be the duty of the Council in such case to recommend to the several Governments concerned what effective military, naval, or air force the Members of the League shall severally contribute to the armed forces to be used to protect the covenants of the League. The Members of the League agree, further, that they will mutually support one another in the financial and economic measures which are taken under this Article, in order to minimise the loss and inconvenience resulting from the above measures, and that they will mutually support one another in resisting any special measures aimed at one of their number by the covenant breaking State, and that they will take the necessary steps to afford passage through their territory to the forces of any of the Members of the League which are co-operating to protect the covenants of the League. Any Member of the League which has violated any covenant of the League may be declared to be no longer a Member of the League by a vote of the Council concurred in by the Representatives of all the other Members of the League represented thereon.

ARTICLE 17.

In the event of a dispute between a Member of the League and a State which is not a Member of the League, or between States not Members of the League, the State or States, not Members of the League shall be invited to accept the obligations of membership in the League for the purposes of such dispute, upon such conditions as the Council may deem just. If such invitation is accepted, the provisions of Articles 12 to 16 inclusive shall be applied with such modifications as may be deemed necessary by the Council. Upon such invitation being given the Council shall immediately institute an inquiry into the circumstances of the dispute and recommend such action as may seem best and most effectual in the circumstances. If a State so invited shall refuse to accept the obligations of membership in the League for the purposes of such dispute, and shall resort to war against a Member of the League, the provisions of Article 16 shall be applicable as against the State taking such action. If both parties to the dispute when so invited refuse to accept the obligations of membership in the League for the purpose of such dispute, the Council may take such measures and make such recommendations as will prevent hostilities and will result in the settlement of the dispute.

ARTICLE 18.

Every treaty or international engagement entered into hereafter by any Member of the League shall be forthwith registered with the Secretariat and shall as soon as possible be published by it. No such treaty or international engagement shall be binding until so registered.

ARTICLE 19.

The Assembly may from time to time advise the reconsideration by Members of the League of treaties which have become inapplicable and the consideration of international conditions whose continuance might endanger the peace of the world.

ARTICLE 20.

The Members of the League severally agree that this Covenant is accepted as abrogating all obligations or understandings inter se which are inconsistent with the terms thereof, and solemnly undertake that they will not hereafter enter into any engagements inconsistent with the terms thereof. In case any Member of the League shall, before becoming a Member of the League, have undertaken any obligations inconsistent with the terms of this Covenant, it shall be the duty of such Member to take immediate steps to procure its release from such obligations.

ARTICLE 21.

Nothing in this Covenant shall be deemed to affect the validity of international engagements, such as treaties of arbitration or regional understandings like the Monroe doctrine, for securing the maintenance of peace.

ARTICLE 22.

To those colonies and territories which as a consequence of the late war have ceased to be under the sovereignty of the States which formerly governed them and which are inhabited by peoples not yet able to stand by themselves under the strenuous conditions of the modern world, there should be applied the principle that the well-being and development of such peoples form a sacred trust of civilisation and that securities for the performance of this trust should be embodied in this Covenant. The best method of giving practical effect to this principle is that the tutelage of such peoples should be entrusted to advanced nations who by reason of their resources, their experience or their geographical position can best undertake this responsibility, and who are willing to accept it, and that this tutelage should be exercised by them as Mandatories on behalf of the League. The character of the mandate must differ according to the stage of the development of the people, the geographical situation of the territory, its economic conditions, and other similar circumstances. Certain communities formerly belonging to the Turkish Empire have reached a stage of development where their existence as independent nations can be provisionally recognised subject to the rendering of administrative advice and assistance by a Mandatory until such time as they are able to stand alone. The wishes of these communities must be a principal consideration in the selection of the Mandatory. Other peoples, especially those of Central Africa, are at such a stage that the Mandatory must be responsible for the administration of the territory under conditions which will guarantee freedom of conscience and religion, subject only to the maintenance of public order and morals, the prohibition of abuses such as the slave trade, the arms traffic, and the liquor traffic, and the prevention of the establishment of fortifications or military and naval bases and of military training of the natives for other than police purposes and the defence of territory, and will also secure equal opportunities for the trade and commerce of other Members of the League. There are territories, such as South-West Africa and certain of the South Pacific Islands, which, owing to the sparseness of their population, or their small size, or their remoteness from the centres of civilisation, or their geographical contiguity to the territory of the Mandatory, and other circumstances, can be best administered under the laws of the Mandatory as integral portions of its territory, subject to the safeguards above mentioned in the interests of the indigenous population. In every case of mandate, the Mandatory shall render to the Council an annual report in reference to the territory committed to its charge. The degree of authority, control, or administration to be exercised by the Mandatory shall, if not previously agreed upon by the Members of the League, be explicitly defined in each case by the Council. A permanent Commission shall be constituted to receive and examine the annual reports of the Mandatories and to advise the Council on all matters relating to the observance of the mandates.

ARTICLE 23.

Subject to and in accordance with the provisions of international conventions existing or hereafter to be agreed upon, the Members of the League: (a) will endeavour to secure and maintain fair and humane conditions of labour for men, women, and children, both in their own countries and in all countries to which their commercial and industrial relations extend, and for that purpose will establish and maintain the necessary international organisations; (b) undertake to secure just treatment of the native inhabitants of territories under their control; (c) will entrust the League with the general supervision over the execution of agreements with regard to the traffic in women and children, and the traffic in opium and other dangerous drugs; (d) will entrust the League with the general supervision of the trade in arms and ammunition with the countries in which the control of this traffic is necessary in the common interest; (e) will make provision to secure and maintain freedom of communications and of transit and equitable treatment for the commerce of all Members of the League. In this connection, the special necessities of the regions devastated during the war of 1914–1918 shall be borne in mind; (f) will endeavour to take steps in matters of international concern for the prevention and control of disease.

ARTICLE 24.

There shall be placed under the direction of the League all international bureaux already established by general treaties if the parties to such treaties consent. All such international bureaux and all commissions for the regulation of matters of international interest hereafter constituted shall be placed under the direction of the League. In all matters of international interest which are regulated by general conventions but which are not placed under the control of international bureaux or commissions, the Secretariat of the League shall, subject to the consent of the Council and if desired by the parties, collect and distribute all relevant information and shall render any other assistance which may be necessary or desirable. The Council may include as part of the expenses of the Secretariat the expenses of any bureau or commission which is placed under the direction of the League.

ARTICLE 25.

The Members of the League agree to encourage and promote the establishment and co-operation of duly authorised voluntary national Red

Cross organisations having as purposes the improvement of health, the prevention of disease, and the mitigation of suffering throughout the world.

ARTICLE 26.

Amendments to this Covenant will take effect when ratified by the Members of the League whose representatives compose the Council and by a majority of the Members of the League whose Representatives compose the Assembly. No such amendment shall bind any Member of the League which signifies its dissent therefrom, but in that case it shall cease to be a Member of the League.

Appendix IV

Inaugural Address
Delivered before the Board of Directors of the Southwestern Presbyterian University

August 17, 1876
by the Rev. Joseph R. Wilson, D.D.,
and Published by Request of the Board,
at its Meeting in June 1886.

Gentlemen of the Board of Directors—

The University which is under your care has attracted the pleased attention of the friends of progressive education throughout the country; and its growing importance is a source of satisfaction to many who have no interest in its prosperity other than that which, in large minds, springs from a gratified public spirit. From a number of our States students have already been attracted to its several schools, and the magnet which has drawn these is destined to be felt throughout a constantly widening circle of influence. It needs not to be said that much of the success which has thus far been achieved, is due to the able Faculty of your selection, at whose head appears the name of one who has the entire confidence of all those to whom it has been given to know how to reverence wisdom, or respect dignity, or recognize eminency. I, therefore, cannot but be conscious of a glow of pardonable pride in view of an official connection with this rising Institution and these superior men.

Yet it has been with the recoil of an unaffected timidity that I have accepted the Professorship upon whose active duties I am soon to enter; even the timidity which, true to the derivation of the word, implies the presence of a certain fear. The shrinking of my apprehensions is, however, not occasioned by the fact that the business of professorial instruction is in itself one to which I have hitherto been unaccustomed. On the contrary, my past life has been greatly enriched by the pleasures of class-room teaching: and I have had abundant opportunity to discover that as no service, when discharged thoroughly, is harder, so when not dispatched perfunctorily, there is one more fascinating. The trepidation to which I confess is, in a large degree, due to quite another consideration; to this: that it is expected of me to fulfill a task which no predecessor has undertaken—to prosecute a journey for which there is no trodden path, and in which my steps are to be those of a pioneer. The work assigned me is a work hitherto wholly untried. Instructors in theology there are many: beginners in this department of knowledge there have been to whom no foregoing preceptor has declared the way, nor is this the only University in connection with which a movement has progressed similar to that on whose threshold we are now standing. Nevertheless, the fact remains that the Church with which you and I are connected—nor any portion of it—has heretofore inaugurated what is now incipient at this place. It is a novelty in the history of Presbyterianism. In advancing this statement, I am not unmindful of those renowned Scotch universities wherein chairs of theology have long been occupied by men of brilliancy and of power—of a theology, too, which is, in all essential respects, distinctively like that of our own. These institutions are, however, of Caesar's headship rather than of Christ's. Nothing that matches them, therefore, would be tolerated in this land of unfettered Christian freedom: nothing that makes the Church a pensioner of the State. The theological "Seminary" we have had in its stead—a species of organization which, until after the Disruption in Scotland, was peculiar to America—and instituted by our Presbyterian fathers at a time when there was no alternative choice: if there was to be a perpetuation of an educated ministry, this wholly novel device seemed indispensable. And some are bold to predict that the hour will, one day, strike when the conventual Seminary plan must be abandoned for something wider and freer, for a plan which shall place students of divinity in contact, at more points than now, with the world around them; as, it might easily be shown, ought to be the case. Certain it is, however, that by the arrangement here making—for putting a course of theology in concurrent connection with the usual schools of a University series—you will be the first in the history of our Church to prepare a practical answer to the question whether there shall be a signal departure from the customary policy. And, whilst it furnishes occasion for gratulation, that the independent enterprise of these Southwestern Synods has thus entered upon a path which is lined upon no guiding chart,—yet, just at this point it is, that my disquietings find their awakening and their foreboding—lest, in such hands as mine, an experiment upon whose success so much may depend should become perplexed and marred, and the skeptical watchers shall have it to say: "Aha! It was not worth the trial." But, happily, there is always to be had the help that descends from the mightiest of all, on whose sustaining arm the humblest of His servants, who does what he can to help himself, may confidently rely. I am sure, too, of encouragement from my brethren, to many of whom I am indebted for such assurances of sympathy and support as might almost serve to embolden cowardice itself. And yet, whatsoever one's upholdings when undergoing such a trust, he must needs be appalled, not alone by reason of the novelty of his position and the peculiar responsibility it involves, but also because of the labor that is required for the mastery of a science which, in addition to its own inherent ambiguities, is constantly pressed with new questions that demand the utmost resources of the very widest scholarship.

There is, however, not a little comfort derivable from the fact that the truths I am to handle are not still awaiting the initiative of an original exploration; for, the patient industry and practiced learning of the past have not merely brought these truths forth into large and distinct view, but, to an extent almost exhaustive, have ascertained their interdependent relations and exhibited many of their finest harmonies. So that, with respect to nearly all of them, there is now needed, not so much the painstaking discoverer, or the inventive systematizer, as the trustful follower and the thoughtful imitator. What, therefore, the occupant of this chair shall lack in brilliancy of adventure among the clouds that may seem to hang upon the horizon of his extensive subject, ought to find its compensation in his conservative hold upon the secure ground of established certainty, where there is room enough, and to spare, for the largest building which intellectual fervor—like that of Thomas Chalmers—ever erected; or speculative fancy—like that of Edward Irving—ever adorned.

But what is this fixed theology, whose bias is at once so broad and so trustworthy? It had been my purpose to select a few of its most vital points, and discuss these somewhat in extenso. But it is better, I think, to indicate in more general description the character of the theology to which it shall be my aim to adhere—regarding it in its entirety, as being less formal and more satisfactory not only, but also because time is thus saved and tedium avoided.

It might, indeed, be sufficient simply to state that the theology to which I am referring is strictly *biblical* in every portion of its structure, and as to the very atmosphere which breathes through it all. Inasmuch, however, as it is a fact that, with scarcely an exception, the many differing theological systems which claim to be evangelical (and even some which can make no such claim) do likewise profess to find their own vindication in what this same Holy Book authorizes, it is necessary to be more explicit.

That theology, then, which I regard as possessing most largely and most distinctly, the seal of a divine warrant, is known to every student of creed-history as the *Pauline*; and whose characteristic features are quite unmistakable, if, for nothing else, by reasons of the very peltings it has received from the numerous foes with which, in every age, it has had to contend. Or, let us style it the theology of the *Reformation*,—as more completely illustrated by brave Zwingle than by bold Luther; as lifted into finer prominence by Knox the hardy than by Cranmer the hesitating; and the cardinal principles of which the agency of undaunted Wickliffe was, long before their day, chosen to revive amid the ashes of an apparently expiring Christianity—whilst now and again such martyrs as the erudite Huss and the eloquent Latimer had it translated for them into those horses of flame, the fire of whose nostrils lights the world to this day.

Or, name it, if you please, the theology of protesting Germany, of covenanting Scotland, of counter-remonstrant Holland, to say nothing of Calvinistic Geneva that modern but improved Athanasian Alexandria—the theology which fed the faith and fanned the hopes and fortified the courage of a "thus-saith-the-Lord" ancestry, the intelligence, the intrepidity, the inspiring activity of whose robust piety have never been excelled—the well-tried theology which now signalizes our unequaled Catechisms and preeminent Confession—and whose most conspicuous glory was, from the first, what it still is, the glory of the *cross*—the theology that has steadfastly refused to tolerate at the altar of a sin-bearing sacrifice, any Priest; or on the throne of redeeming sovereignty, any King; or within the sanctuary of the soul itself, any Prophet—who shall shadow however dimly, or rival, however distantly, the all-sufficient Lord Jesus Christ, apart from whom, whether viewed in His voluntary humiliation or in His wonderful exaltation, no sinner can ever be saved and no believer can ever be sainted. It is that theology, therefore, the central facts of which are the creation of man, his fall in the representative first, and his recover in the vicarious second, Adam: —and these surrounded by a circle of doctrines wherein emerges the necessity for repentance, for a new birth, for union with Christ, for the indwelling Spirit, for entire sanctification through appointed means of grace—to say nothing of that surprising eschatology which discloses the mystery of death, declares the millennium, depicts the final judgment, divides the curtain beyond which are beheld the raptures of heaven and the regrets of hell, the one the perfection of happiness because the perfection of holiness, the other the perfection of grief because the perfection of guilt. It is that theology, moreover, which is at once a proclamation of man's personal responsibility because of his free agency, and of God's absolute universal rule because of His essential supremacy: —the theology which publishes, without attempting to explain, the unity of the God-head as immanent in three co-equal persons, and to view their several self-distributed places in the completed plan of redeeming love: —the whole issuing in a visible Church, whose members, entering by baptism, and composed of professing believers and their offspring, are known to belong to the invisible Church by the visible fruits of their holy living.

Such, then, (with omissions some of which are inferentially suppliable, and others which, being left out, do not affect the general portraiture) is a sketch of that grand theology which is familiar and precious to the thoughts of all those biblical experts who are neither Prelatist nor Independent, Arminian nor Socinian, Antinomian nor

Legalist, Formalist nor Fatalist; Quietist nor Rationalist: —a theology
which is also a philanthropy, but which is not a mere philosophy or
a mere morality: —and which, at every point, rests upon that infallible Scripture from whose arbitrament there is no appeal as for whose
authority there is no substitute: consequently a theology from whose
well defined paths if your professor shall at any time swerve, let him
be promptly silenced, for you will not dare to absolve him, "though he
were an angel from heaven."

What then? Why, this: your voice unites with mine in a plea for
conservatism, the maintenance, unimpaired, of that great body of
sacred lessons which has been given into our hands by the orthodox
belief of many preceding generations as an invaluable deposit, freely
to profit by but never to be profaned. Nor need we fear that thus
we shall lay the grasp of arrest upon and shackle the limbs of our
Church's advancement in whatsoever direction she may propose to
move for the spiritual subdual of the world. That doctrinal conserva-
tion is not inconsistent with practical aggressiveness, let the entire
history of Presbyterian exploit, in every field of controversy and of
conquest, loudly attest. Or, if the lack of readiness as to our forward
works has sometimes seemed to throw discredit upon the calm repose
of our faith, the blame is not traceable to a fettered theology only to
a frozen piety. At any rate, in these later fermenting days, when the
temptations are so sharp and so imperative, to indulge in sensational
departures from "the faith which was once (*i.e.* once for all) delivered
to the saints," the conviction cannot be impressed too strongly upon
our minds, that alone by walking "in the good old paths" is there
either ultimate safety or present satisfaction. Every qualified theological preceptor may, indeed, be permitted to elaborate in his own idio-
syncratic way the several truths of which he shall treat, just as the
competent preacher, to quiet the demands that are constantly being
made for newer moulds of thought, may be allowed to enforce his pulpit themes by conformable methods of illustration. But it is one thing
to alter a superannuated fashion of doctrinal *dress*—although even
this requires to be done with shears of caution—and quite another
to repair the texture of the cloth itself, as if this, too, were worn out.
The gold of divine things may sometimes, when the dust of ages is
dimming it, be freshly polished; but, in the process, there must be no

portion of its precious mass rubbed away. The oldest established and truest theology may, without detriment, be occasionally submitted to the alembic of hitherto untried tests; but never when the least waste shall thereby occur. It is no foe to a fertile fancy that would only decorate it; but its wise friends will not consent to any material change in the effort to reform it. The originality which shall sustain it with fresh arguments is to be welcomed, but the originality which, not content with this, proceeds to clip or to mend it is to be warned off. The ark of God may be put into a "new cart," as when it was brought out of Abinadab's house; but it needs no anxious Uzzah, with the plausible hand, to prevent the appointed oxen from shaking it.

And precisely here emerges a weighty reason for imparting to our future ministry a thorough theological training—not alone that they thus may be transfused with the great principles they are to expound and impress, but that they may so be informed by these as composing an articulated *system*, at the sight of whose beauty they shall be the less incited to the bad work of tampering with it. Heresy is a malaria that may float in the purest air. Not often, however, is heresy the offspring of a sound and comprehensive scholarship. Nearly always it is the fruit of ignorance—an effect due to a limited horizon. The apostles themselves to what errors were they not prone before their minds were fully enlightened! What a difference between Peter the petulant denier, and Peter the Pentecost preacher or the epistle-writer; or between John shrinking from the shadow of the cross and John the apocalyptic seer; or between Saul the Old Testament harpy and Paul the New Testament hero! Those men who, in every age of the Church, have aspired to be teachers before they themselves had been adequately taught—it has been as a miracle when, if possessed of constructive genius or of vivid imagination, they have not become heretics almost as soon as they became heralds: the bringers in of false doctrines, to which in all sincerity perhaps, they were ready to swear, because they were not familiar with the mightier true. You will find, therefore, that it has not usually been the chair where solid learning sits a sound theology has had the most to fear. Sciolism is the mother of that presumption which refuses to "let the well-enough alone"; and it is the very arrogance of presumption that essays to reconstruct those time honored standards of ours which, having done successful battle upon so many of the high places of contention, continue as bright and unimpaired as ever they were, are indeed all the brighter and the better because of the blows they have received and withstood.

But, it may now be asked, does conservatism in theology forbid that this great science shall, to any great extent, be *progressive*, requiring that it must always remain at a standstill just where we find it, without the possibility of accretion or of that power of growth which belongs to all things that live? Is it already perfect, and thus susceptible of no manner or degree of improvement? Has it put forth all its branches or perfected all its buds? No thoughtful man will reply to such questionings by an unqualified affirmative answer. We are, indeed, bound to believe that the cardinal tenets of Christianity admit of no modification whatsoever, seeing that they are the manifest product of infallible wisdom. But who will venture to say that the time shall never come—that a clearer day shall never dawn—when some of these shall be better *understood* than they are at present? And with an advancing elucidation, the science whose office it is to make known, not to create, must of course advance with equal step. Thus, the measure of "progress" to which our existing theology can properly look forward, must be due to a deeper insight into inspired Scripture itself—an insight which may issue in requiring a less inadequate statement of the obscurer doctrines, whilst producing a still livelier persuasion of what is fundamental, along with a broader comprehension of the whole articulated body of sacred truth. Improved exegetical apparatus, in a word, is likely to achieve almost every desirable result: whether in showing the Bible to be nowhere inconsistent with itself; or in displaying its accord with the established facts that illustrate natural law; or in winning from its foes so much of debatable ground as may yet, on this hand or on that, remain as an object of dispute. That is, accepting the existing Scripture canon, as we demonstrately must, and as it has been accepted by evangelical Christendom from the first, *ubique, semper, ab omnibus;* and resting, as also we unhesitatingly must, upon the evidence of its divine and literal inspiration, the principal call which is made upon modern scholarship is for rendering more perspicuous, here and there, the exact meaning of the finished Scripture's original wording. So far, therefore, as the science of theology includes the ever-extending science of *interpretation*, it is progressive, and no further than this.

We need, accordingly, nothing of such "higher criticism," which, not content with illuminating the purport, with ascertaining the precise sense of God's word, audaciously suggests an altogether different word, by dint of denying its theopneustic integrity and by the wild endeavor to reduce to a rank with the merely apocryphal, the Pentateuch even, to substitute for this keying portion of the mighty arch of revelation certain dream-fictions of its own. *High* criticism this! It is not genuine criticism at all—which, when true, occupies the attitude of a witness not that of a lawgiver, of a historian not of an oracle—at any rate, is not a specious defamer of the truth it professes, however loosely, to hold, but only its honest declarer; or else its surrender altogether, which in these days much of what is called the best criticism actually is.

Having thus said enough for justifying my occupancy of the chair to which I have been assigned—if such justification be found in the sincere heartiness of an unreserved subscription to those standards of our Presbyterian orthodoxy which, in the future as in the past, are to be regarded as unchangeable, except in the one open direction of an enlarging knowledge of its various contents—I am now about to relieve your attention, leaving unsaid much more that might be permitted, in the way of expanding or of illustrating what has been so partially discussed.

Only, before resuming my seat, I will take the liberty of inviting your thoughts, for a few moments, to a question of importance which was purposely left unnoticed when adverting to the hopeful fact that you are beginning in this University a new era in theological education—by no longer isolating it, as has been the case with our Church heretofore, and still is elsewhere. Is it exhaustive of your design to furnish a convenience for the study of theology to those *only* who shall have the gospel ministry in their professional prospect? This I presume it must mainly be, but not, I trust, exclusively. For, let me ask, has not the time come—nay, did it not come much earlier than now—when the immense science of which I have been speaking ought not to be regarded as, in view of a complete education, essentially different from the sciences, say, of law and medicine and engineering? Ought it to be longer classed with the merely technical or the purely vocational? All persons have occasion, now and then, to heal the sick, or even to prepare a case at law, or to project a road, but who is not always in need of a sound theology upon a knowledge of which he is, at every turn of life, dependent—dependent at the very core and centre of his being—and by the light of which his very eternity is illumined? It would, of course, not be possible to instruct fully the multitudes in this branch of necessary learning. These must obtain what they can, as they can, of its easier lessons from friendly neighbor or faithful preacher, or fingered Bible: and, thank God, they do, many of them by one means or another, find the right way amid a thousand obstacles. Yet, suppose there were a large and ever enlarging class of persons—merchants, farmers, physicians, politicians, lawyers—who, scattered through the land, should be so versed in the truths of a theology like ours as to be competent to indoctrinate others also, or, at the least, to guard, where occasion offered, against unsuspected error, what a new face society must by and by wear! How much stronger, too, would be our churches, with men in the pew as able perhaps as the men in the pulpit, to apprehend and to expound the messages of saving love! Nor would infidelity have so free a field, when laics, such as the late Judge Black, as well as clerics, were, leader-like, championing the cause of God—the layman being, indeed, all the mightier because of his supposed more disinterested and unpaid volunteering.

But, however all this may be, it has, in my judgment, become well-nigh indispensable: the addition to a liberal education of a theological schooling, which is the placing of a roof upon the otherwise unfinished scholarly house, if not of an essential bracing wall to hold it up and to make it habitable. Or, to change the figure, the ordinary scholarship, however complete and heavily freighted, will, without this balancing adjunct, run always as an endangered ship, upon its beam-ends, to be wrecked, perhaps, at last.

Let the departure you are making to be a great one—the greatest possible—and the voice of it go forth as an invitation to all young men to resort hither for a training the most thorough that can be obtained, if they will accept *theology* as the finish to their classics, as not *here*, at least, an *esoteric* study to be imparted to the inner few whilst denied to the outside many. But, enough.

I had a dear friend who, an honored theological professor during a decade of highly useful years, and completed just before he passed to his reward, entered upon his duties with a trembling solicitude similar to that which is a part of my experience to-day. I allude to the Rev. Dr. A. B. VanZandt: the closing words, slightly altered, of whose inaugural address, delivered at New Brunswick in 1872, I fittingly adopt as my own:

> Immediate results that shall meet the desires and gladden the heart of the Church, are more than I can promise. The issue is with God; and, without the advantage of a name of reputation in this new field of labor, I must cast myself upon His grace, and upon the forbearance of His people. To my brethren in the ministry, and especially to those by whose influence and suffrages this responsibility has been laid upon me, I claim the right to appeal. And, by all their personal regards, by their attachment to this young institution, the prosperity of which is identified with that of the Church in whose ranks we together serve her adorable Head, I importune them, whilst I utter the earnest and utmost desire of a burdened heart in those touching and comprehensive words of an apostle: "brethren, pray for us."

Notes

Introduction

1 John Maynard Keynes, *The Economic Consequences of the Peace* (New York: Harper & Row, 1920), 42.

2 John Milton Cooper, *The Warrior and the Priest* (Cambridge, Mass.: Harvard University Press, 1983), 19.

3 John Milton Cooper, *Breaking the Heart of the World, Woodrow Wilson and the Fight for the League of Nations* (Cambridge: Cambridge University Press, 2001).

4 Niels Aage Thorsen, *The Political Thought of Woodrow Wilson, 1875–1910* (Princeton: Princeton University Press, 1988), 237–38.

5 John A. Thompson, *Woodrow Wilson: Profiles in Power* (London/New York: Longman, 2002), 249.

6 Jan Willem Schulte Nordholt, *Woodrow Wilson: A Life for World Peace* (Los Angeles: University of California Press, 1991), 41–42.

7 Arthur S. Link, *Woodrow Wilson: A Brief Biography* (Cleveland: World Publishing, 1963), 64–65.

8 John M. Mulder, *Woodrow Wilson: The Years of Preparation* (Princeton: Princeton University Press, 1978).

9 N. Gordon Levin Jr., *Woodrow Wilson and World Politics* (New York: Oxford University Press, 1968).

10 Robert S. McNamara and James G. Blight, *Wilson's Ghost* (New York: Public Affairs, 2001).

11 Thomas William Lamont, April 1, 1919, in *The Papers of Woodrow Wilson*, ed. Arthur S. Link, 60 vols. (Princeton: Princeton University Press, 1966–1978), vol. 56, 502. (Hereafter *PWW*)

12 Lloyd E. Ambrosius, *Wilsonianism: Woodrow Wilson and His Legacy in American Foreign Relations* (New York: Palgrave Macmillan, 2002).

13   P. C. Kemeny, *Princeton in the Nation's Service, Religious Ideals and Educational Practice, 1868–1928* (New York: Oxford University Press, 1998).

14   Edwin A. Weinstein, *Woodrow Wilson: A Medical and Psychological Biography* (Princeton: Princeton University Press, 1981); and Kendrick A. Clements, *Woodrow Wilson: World Statesman* (Chicago: Ivan R. Dee, 1999).

15   Thomas J. Knock, *To End All Wars: Woodrow Wilson and the Quest for a New World Order* (New York: Oxford University Press, 1992); Daniel D. Stid, *The President as Statesman: Woodrow Wilson and the Constitution* (Lawrence: University Press of Kansas, 1998); Phyllis Lee Levin, *Edith and Woodrow* (New York: Scribner, 2001); Margaret MacMillan, *Paris 1919: Six Months that Changed the World* (New York: Random House, 2001).

16   *PWW*, vol. 41, 452–53.

17   Andrew Preston, "Bridging the Gap between the Sacred and the Secular in the History of American Foreign Relations." *The Journal of the Society for Historians of American Foreign Relations* 30, no. 5 (2006): 783–812.

18   Among these are authors Michael Lerner, Jim Wallis, Randall Balmer, Robin Meyers, and others who have weighed in on the subject of the persistence of faith in American politics.

Chapter 1

1   Frederic Yates, March 4, 1913, in *PWW*, vol. 27, 155.

2   Link, *Woodrow Wilson*, 27.

3   Woodrow Wilson, "Remarks in London to Free Church Leaders," December 28, 1918, in *PWW*, vol. 53, 530.

4   For a further discussion on Joseph Wilson and the specifics of both his theology and the influence he had on his son, see John Mulder, "Joseph Ruggles Wilson: Southern Presbyterian Patriarch," *Journal of Presbyterian History* 52 (1974): 245–71.

5   Ray Stannard Baker, *Woodrow Wilson Life and Letters, Youth 1856–1890* (Garden City, N.Y.: Doubleday, 1927), 1.

6   The official name of the new denomination founded in J. R. Wilson's church was "The Presbyterian Church in the Confederate States of America." Later, after the war, it became the PCUS.

7   Mulder, "Joseph Ruggles Wilson," 10.

8   Mark Noll, *The Princeton Theology, 1812–1921* (Grand Rapids: Baker Book House, 1983), 14. Hodge has until recently been an assigned text in conservative Presbyterian seminaries.

9   Shorthand Diary, September 10, 1876, in *PWW*, vol. 1, 191.

10   Confidential Journal, December 28, 1889, in *PWW*, vol. 6, 462–63.

11   Further reading, Noll, *The Princeton Theology*.

12   Two news reports of an address in New York, November 19, 1905, in *PWW*, vol. 16, 228, 230.

13   Cooper, *Warrior and the Priest*, 19.
14   Perhaps the most thorough argument against placing any importance on religious influence when examining Wilson's politics is Thorsen's, *The Political Thought of Woodrow Wilson, 1875–1910*. Thorsen demonstrates the problem secular historians face in making the connection between Wilson's religion and his political thought. He argues that the word *covenant* was not a religious concept in Wilson's mind because his religious background was Pauline and not Abrahamic. The Presbyterian idea of *covenant*, however, was both Pauline and Abrahamic. Thorsen's secular prejudice is even more evident when he argues that ascribing importance to Wilson's religion makes him *premodern* and takes away from the substance of his modern political thought. This line of argument does not take Wilson's intellectual antinomy into account, projects a sacred/secular divide that did not exist in Wilson's mind and displays a *modern* prejudice against placing any substantial importance upon religious belief in Wilson's political language. The evidence from Wilson's private writings, the private writings of those who knew him and the overall course of his life argues against this approach.
15   John Boldt, *A Free Church, A Holy Nation: Abraham Kuyper's American Public Theology* (Grand Rapids: Wm. B. Eerdmans, 2001), 136.
16   See Boldt, *A Free Church.*
17   "Of the Study of Politics," November 25, 1886, in *PWW*, vol. 5, 399.
18   J. R. Wilson, letter, March 12, 1887, in *PWW*, vol. 5, 467.
19   Wilson, "Calvin–Geneva, France," April 14, 1887, in *PWW*, vol. 5, 488. This was not unique to Wilson. Calvin's theology has always been paired with political philosophy. Michael Walzer wrote a thorough study on this called *The Revolution of the Saints* (Cambridge, Mass.: Harvard University Press, 1965) and for a more recent citation, see Duncan Forrester, *Martin Luther and John Calvin*, in Leo Strauss and Joseph Cropsey, eds., *History of Political Philosophy* (Chicago: University of Chicago Press, 1987), 318–55.
20   Wilson, "Calvin–Geneva," April 14, 1887, in *PWW*, vol. 5, 488–90.
21   Wilson, "Calvin–Geneva," April 14, 1887, in *PWW*, vol. 5, 488–90.
22   "Inaugural Address," January 15, 1885, December 17, 1884, in *PWW*, vol. 3, 549, 612–13. Delivered before the board of directors of the Southwestern Presbyterian Seminary, June 1885, Rhodes College archives, Memphis, Tenn.
23   The Westminster Confession of Faith.
24   Joseph Wilson, "Inaugural Address," June 1885 in *Woodrow Wilson Papers, Library of Congress (WWPLC)*.
25   Confidential Journal, December 29, 1889, in *PWW*, vol. 6, 463–64.
26   Henry Wilkinson Bragdon, *Woodrow Wilson: The Academic Years* (Cambridge, Mass.: Harvard University Press, 1967), 299.
27   "Political Liberty," December 28, 1889, in *PWW*, vol. 6, 463–64.

28 John Calvin, *Institutes of the Christian Religion,* book 2 (Philadelphia: Westminster Press, 1960), 369–76.

29 A further discussion of this is found in W. Fred Graham, *The Constructive Revolutionary: John Calvin and His Socio-Economic Impact* (Lansing: Michigan State University Press, 1987).

30 Address in Denver on the Bible, May 7, 1911, in *PWW,* vol. 23, 12–20.

31 "Political Liberty," December 28, 1889, in *PWW,* vol. 6, 464.

32 Harley Notter, *The Origins of the Foreign Policy of Woodrow Wilson* (Baltimore: The Johns Hopkins Press, 1937), 16.

33 For further examination of this concept, see Mulder, *Woodrow Wilson,* chap. 1. Also Walzer, *Revolution of the Saints.* Two further works which detail this theological pattern are O. Palmer Robertson, *The Christ of the Covenants* (Phillipsburg, N.J.: Presbyterian and Reformed Publishing, 1980); and David F. Wells, ed., *Southern Reformed Theology* (Grand Rapids: Baker Book House, 1989).

34 Mulder, *Woodrow Wilson,* xiii.

35 Joseph Wilson, like his contemporaries spent much time teaching on the order brought about by the gospel covenant. Many of his handwritten manuscripts remain in the Library of Congress and the Presbyterian Historical Society Archives, *The Heavenly Farmer, Follow Me, James 1:25* in *WWPLC,* reel 523.

36 Mulder, *Woodrow Wilson,* 7–9.

37 Joseph R. Wilson, "The Sun of Righteousness," June 13, 1880, sermon manuscript; "The Heavenly Farmer," 1882, sermon manuscript, in *WWPLC,* reel 523.

38 J. I. Packer, *Evangelism and the Sovereignty of God* (Downers Grove, Ill.: InterVarsity, 1961), 18–19.

39 Another concept which parallels antinomy in Calvinist theology is the idea of *concursus.* This describes a cooperative dualism between two ideas which both explain something but which are in harmony together. This was developed among the Princeton Theologians, particularly Wilson's contemporary at Princeton Seminary, Benjamin Warfield. While both of these dualisms are present in Wilson, the idea of antinomy seems to better explain the inner intellectual conflicts which Wilson demonstrated. Wilson's British political contemporary Arthur J. Balfour, a student of theology and philosophy in his own right, spoke of another version of this concept in his first set of Gifford Lectures when he referred to the doctrine of congruity. Balfour tied it into his overall understanding of how people arrive at belief. He argued that this manner of theological thought produced progress through the interaction of competing ideas. For further examination of this doctrine of congruity, see Arthur J. Balfour, *Theism and Humanism* (Seattle: Inkling Books, 2000), 143–52. For a further examination of the doctrine of concursus,

see Louis Berkhof, *Systematic Theology* (Grand Rapids: Wm. B. Eerdmans, 1991); Benjamin B. Warfield, *Calvin's Doctrine of Creation: The Works of Benjamin B. Warfield,* vol. 5 (New York: Oxford University Press, 1931).

40   See "Political Liberty," December 28, 1889, in *PWW,* vol. 6, 464.

41   Joseph Wilson, "Inaugural Address," June 1885, in *WWPLC.*

42   Joseph Wilson, "Sermon on Malachi 3:17," date uncertain, in *WWPLC.*

43   "Political Liberty," December 28, 1889, in *PWW,* vol. 6, 464.

44   For a study of this type of thinking among evangelicals in America, see Christian Smith, *American Evangelicalism: Embattled and Thriving* (Chicago: University of Chicago Press, 1998). Smith speaks of a concept which he calls "voluntary absolutism" which sheds light on one way this type of thinking is expressed.

45   Charles W. Thompson, *Presidents I Have Known and Two Near Presidents* (Indianapolis: Bobbs-Merrill, 1929), 261.

46   "Political Liberty," December 28, 1889, in *PWW,* vol. 6, 464.

47   Letter to Ellen Axson, October 30, 1883, in *PWW,* vol. 2, 499–505.

48   "Mere Literature," June 17, 1893, in *PWW,* vol. 8, 240–52.

49   Wilson's views on language as a method of governing as well as how he saw inspired leadership using this in Government can be found in his essay, "Government by Debate" (1882), in *PWW,* vol. 2, 159–275. A particular look at section IV dealing with Webster, Calhoun, and Clay demonstrates Wilson's thought on this pattern. Other examples are found in much of Wilson's writing on both leaders, such as "Mr. Gladstone, A Character Sketch" (1880), in *PWW,* vol. 1, 624–42; also "Leaders of Men" (1889), in *PWW,* vol. 6, 646–71.

50   "A Christian Statesman," September 1, 1876, in *PWW,* vol. 1, 188; "The Ideal Statesman," January 30, 1877, in *PWW,* vol. 1, 244.

51   "Work Day Religion," August 11, 1876, in *PWW,* vol. 1, 176–78.

52   "Christ's Army." August 17, 1876, in *PWW,* vol. 1, 180–81.

53   Joseph R. Wilson, "I Tim. 4:12, Believers," Unpublished sermon, ca. 1870–1880, in *WWPLC.*

54   Ephesians 6:10-20.

55   Joseph R. Wilson, "Believers."

56   Joseph R. Wilson, "1 John 3:2," Wilmington 1874, in *WWPLC.*

57   1 Chronicles 12:32.

58   To Ellen, October 30, 1883, in *PWW,* vol. 2, 499–505.

59   "The Ideal Statesman." Compare to "Believers," in *WWPLC.*

60   To Ellen, February 24, 1885, in *PWW,* vol. 4, 287.

61   "A Christian Statesman"; "The Ideal Statesman."

62   "Christian Statesman."

63   Keynes, *Economic Consequences,* 43.

64   Shorthand Diary, June 3, 1877, in *PWW,* vol. 1, 272.

65   Henry F. May, *Protestant Churches and Industrial America* (New York: Harper & Brothers, 1949), 230.

66   The Great Commission calls Christians to "make disciples" of all the nations. That act involved the kind of instruction implied in Isaiah 2, "teaching the nations." By the nineteenth century the term disciple was both a noun and a verb. "The Chinese students were 'discipled' by the missionary." This is an important concept for Wilson, if not an important word, in that he often tried as president to teach (disciple) the nations in democracy. It makes more sense that he derived this idea from the Bible than from Pericles.

67   "The Ministry and the Individual," November 2, 1909, in *PWW*, vol. 19, 477.

68   "The Present Task of the Ministry," May 26, 1909, in *PWW*, vol. 19, 215–22.

69   "The Present Task of the Ministry," 218.

70   "The Ministry and the Individual," 472. Emphasis mine.

71   "The Ministry and the Individual," 478.

72   "The Nature of the State and Its Relationship to Progress," July 2, 1894, in *PWW*, vol. 8, 597–608.

73   "Self Government in France," September 4, 1879, in *PWW*, vol. 1, 515–39.

74   "Self Government in France."

75   Letter to the editor, "Anti Sham," January 25, 1882, in *PWW*, vol. 2, 98–102.

76   Letter to the editor, "Anti Sham," January 25, 1882, in *PWW*, vol. 2, 98.

77   "The Minister and the Community," March 30, 1906, *PWW*, vol. 16, 347, 352.

78   House, *Diary*, November 14, 1914, in "Papers of E. M. House," Yale Archives.

79   House, *Diary*, November 25, December 16, 1914.

80   Consider Woodrow Wilson's views on Romans 13.

81   This view is elaborated in Ernest Lee Tuveson, *Redeemer Nation: The Idea of America's Millenial Role* (Chicago: University of Chicago Press, 1968). See also Michael Peters, "The Politicization of Jonathan Edwards' Millennialism," unpublished Ph.D. diss., St. Louis University, 2000. Two other works on this subject are Gerald McDermott, *One Holy Happy Society: The Public Theology of Jonathan Edwards* (University Park: Pennsylvania State University Press, 1992); and Michael Mooney, "Millennialism and Antichrist in New England, 1630-1760," unpublished Ph.D. diss., Syracuse University, 1982.

82   Letter to Harriett Woodrow, May 10, 1881, in *PWW*, vol. 2, 64.

83   Woodrow Wilson, *A History of the American People,* vol. 5 (New York: Harper & Brothers, 1901), chap. 2, "Return to Normal Conditions," 115–31, chap. 3, "The End of a Century," 299–300.

84 "Address in Jersey City," May 25, 1912, in *PWW*, vol. 24, 443–44.
85 "Leaders of Men," June 17, 1890, in *PWW*, vol. 6, 644–71.
86 Note discussion of Matthew Arnold, June 17, 1890, in *PWW*, vol. 6, 662.
87 Jeremiah 31:33, Romans 2:15, Hebrews 8:10.
88 Woodrow Wilson to Ellen Axson, February 15, 1885, in *PWW*, vol. 4, 255.
89 Joseph Tumulty, *Woodrow Wilson as I Know Him* (Garden City: Doubleday, 1921), chap. 40.
90 "Confidential Journal," December 28, 1889, in *PWW*, vol. 6, 462–63.
91 "The Ideals of America," December 26, 1901, in *PWW*, vol. 12, 208–27.
92 "Religion and Patriotism," July 4, 1902, in *PWW*, vol. 12, 474–78.
93 Wilson, *History of the American People,* vol. 5, 300.
94 "An Address on Patriotism to the Washington Association of New Jersey," February 23, 1903, in *PWW*, vol. 14, 371.
95 "Youth and Christian Progress," November 20, 1905, in *PWW*, vol. 16, 228, 230.
96 "Address in Detroit," September 19, 1912, in *PWW*, vol. 25, 197.

Chapter 2

1 E. M. House [note to Wilson], December 19, 1912, in *PWW,* vol. 25, 614; February 23, 1913, in *PWW,* vol. 27, 128; April 1, 1913, in *PWW,* vol. 27, 253.
2 It would seem that any international peace initiative not paved with plenty of alcohol was doomed from the start.
3 March 5, 1913, in *PWW*, vol. 27, 153–54.
4 To Mary Allen Hulbert, March 9, 1913, in *PWW*, vol. 27, 166–67.
5 "Political Liberty," December 28, 1889, in *PWW*, vol. 6, 464.
6 To Hulbert, March 16, 1913, in *PWW*, vol. 27, 189–90.
7 "Address to Spanish War Veterans," September 10, 1912, in *PWW*, vol. 25, 131.
8 "Inaugural Address," March 4, 1913, in *PWW*, vol. 27, 148.
9 "Address on Jury Reform," May 2, 1913, in *PWW*, vol. 27, 387.
10 November 20, 1905, in *PWW*, vol. 16, 228, 230.
11 "Inaugural Address," March 4, 1913, in *PWW*, vol. 27, 148–52.
12 "Inaugural Address."
13 "Address on Jury Reform," 390.
14 "Address to the Pittsburgh YMCA," October 24, 1914, in *PWW,* vol. 31, 221. The speech should be looked at in its entirety as it displays this aspect of Wilson's approach to the presidency. It is also illuminating in regard to his views on task and character which have been dealt with in connection to May and Cooper earlier in this work.

15 Michael H. Hunt, *The Making of a Special Relationship: The United States and China to 1914* (New York: Columbia University Press, 1983), 217.

16 Letter to Bryan, February, 24, 1913, in *PWW*, vol. 27, 124.

17 Letter to Cleveland Dodge, March 10, 1913, in *PWW*, vol. 27, 167.

18 Edward Jenkins, March 14, 17, 1913, in *PWW*, vol. 27, 179, 190.

19 To John R. Mott, March 21, 1913, in *PWW*, vol. 27, 202.

20 Wilson kept the pressure on Mott. He eventually served on the Mexican commission, became general secretary of the National War Work council and in 1917 was a member of the Special Diplomatic Mission to Russia.

21 Josephus Daniels, *Diary*, March 11, 1913, in *PWW*, vol. 27, 169–70.

22 Daniels, *Diary*, in *PWW*, vol. 27, 170.

23 "Address to the New York Southern Society," December 17, 1912, in *PWW*, vol. 25, 593.

24 "Statement on Relations with Latin America," March 12, 1913, in *PWW*, vol. 27, 172.

25 An example of this is United Fruit Company, which gained influence in Guatemala by working as a de facto "shadow government" to the successive Guatemalan dictatorships. Paul Dosal, *Doing Business With the Dictators: A Political History of United Fruit in Guatemala, 1899–1944* (Wilmington, Del.: Scholarly Resources Books, 1993).

26 House, *Diary*, April 1, 1913.

27 Wilson, *History of the American People*, vol. 4, 122.

28 Wilson, *History of the American People*, vol. 5, 275, 270–72, 273; *PWW*, vol. 25, 130.

29 1 Corinthians 13, note Wilson's language in "Address In Jersey City," May 25, 1912, *PWW*, vol. 24, 443.

30 Clements, *Woodrow Wilson*, 127.

31 Two works detailing the complications in much greater detail are: Robert Quirk, *An Affair of Honor* (Lexington: University of Kentucky Press, 1961); and for a specific look at how Wilson worked out his covenantal theology in practice with Mexico, Mark Benbow, "Leading Them to the Promised Land," unpublished Ph.D. diss., Ohio University, 1999. For an eyewitness account see Edith O'Shaughnessy, *Intimate Pages of Mexican History* (New York: George H. Doran, 1920) and *A Diplomat's Wife in Mexico* (New York: Harper & Brothers, 1916).

32 Letter to Ellen, July 27, 1913, in *PWW*, vol. 28, 85.

33 Quoted in Quirk, *An Affair of Honor*. See also O'Shaughnessy, *A Diplomat's Wife*; idem., *Papers Relating to the Foreign Relations of the United States, 1914*, vol. 1 (Washington, Government Printing Office, 1931), 443–85.

34 Wilson to Hale, April 19, 1913, in *PWW*, vol. 27, 335.

35 Charles W. Thompson, *Presidents I Have Known*, 261.

36 Lind, on turning down the ambassadorship to Sweden, stated that he wanted to contribute something to the "redemption of our state." June 12, 1913, in *PWW*, vol. 27, 514.

37 "Self Government in France," in *PWW*, vol. 1, 515–39.

38 Conversations with Cecil Spring Rice, in *PWW*, vol. 29, 228–33. Clements, *Woodrow Wilson*, 127. Bryan and Wilson were concerned about the involvement of the Church in the political process as they feared it would create yet another division between clerical and anticlerical forces that Wilson had described as existing in France (*PWW*, vol. 28, 325–26).

39 Tyrrell to Grey, November 14, 1913, in *PWW*, vol. 28, 544.

40 Wilson's complicated relationship with the peace movements at the beginning of his presidency is examined in Calvin DeArmond Davis, *The United States and the Second Hague Peace Conference, American Diplomacy and International Organization 1899–1914* (Durham, N.C.: Duke University Press, 1975), 327–38.

41 *PWW*, vol. 25, 131. Ephesians 6:12: "For our struggle is not against enemies of blood and flesh, but against the rulers, against the authorities, against the cosmic powers of this present darkness, against the spiritual forces of evil in the heavenly places."

42 Wilson, "Address in Denver on the Bible," May 7, 1911, in *PWW*, vol. 23, 14–15.

43 On the subject of just war as Wilson understood it, see Benbow, "Leading them to the Promised Land," 46–54. For Pauline theology on the role of government, as Wilson's contemporaries would have understood it, see Herman Ridderbos, *Paul: An Outline of His Theology* (Grand Rapids: Wm. B. Eerdmans, 1975), 320–26.

44 Remarks to National Press Club, May 15, 1916; *PWW*, vol. 37, 48.

45 House, *Diary*, August 30, 1914.

46 Five telegrams from Hale, November 14, 1913, in *PWW*, vol. 28, 541–43.

47 House, *Diary*, August 30, 1914. Also see "Constitutional Government," March 24, 1908, in *PWW*, vol. 18, 114.

48 January 8, 1915, in *PWW*, vol. 32.

49 House, *Diary*, November 12, 1913; also *PWW*, vol. 28, 531.

50 See Wilson's recorded speech, "On the Trusts," September 24, 1912, from *In Their Own Voices: The U.S. Presidential Elections of 1908 and 1912* (Marston Records, 2000).

51 Quirk, *An Affair of Honor*, 17–18.

52 "Statement on the Chinese Loan," *PWW*, vol. 27, 192–94.

53 William H. Taft, "Fourth State of the Union Address to Congress," December 3, 1912.

54 December 28, 1912, in *PWW*, vol. 25, 629.

55 "The Banker and the Nation," September 30, 1908, in *PWW*, vol. 18, 426–30.

56 "Address to Mary Baldwin Seminary," December 28, 1912, in *PWW*, vol. 25, 629.

57 "Address on Latin America Policy," in *PWW*, vol. 28, 448.

58 *PWW*, vol. 28, 450.

59 *PWW*, vol. 28, 451.

60 *PWW*, Vol. 28, 452.

61 See Quirk, *An Affair of Honor*.

62 Draft of a Circular Note to the Powers, October 24, 1913, in *PWW*, vol. 28, 431.

63 Bryan to Lind, December 13, 1913, in *PWW*, vol. 29, 34.

64 Exchanges between Hale, Bryan, and Wilson, November 16–17, 1913, in *PWW*, vol. 28, 557–62. See also, Clements, *Woodrow Wilson*, 127.

65 Spring Rice to Grey, February 7, 1914, in *PWW*, vol. 29, 230.

66 Exchange between Spring Rice and Grey, February 7, 1914, in *PWW*, vol. 29, 228–33.

67 Exchange between Spring Rice and Grey, February 7, 1914, in *PWW*, vol. 29, 230.

68 Interview with Samuel Blythe, April 27, 1914, in *PWW*, vol. 29, 521.

69 To Bryan, April 11, 1914, in *PWW*, vol. 29, 421.

70 *PWW*, vol. 29, 421.

71 This pattern had precipitated the resignation of John Bassett Moore, the most distinguished living American international lawyer and the previous State Department counselor. Spring Rice, who admired Moore's grasp of international law, commented that he was often bypassed when the president wanted advice and many matters of U.S. policy were withheld from him (February 2, 1914, in *PWW*, vol. 29, 215–16).

72 Charles W. Thompson, *Presidents I Have Known,* 261.

73 House, *Diary,* April 16, 1914; also *PWW*, vol. 29, 449.

74 Wilson had permanent loss of vision in his left eye following the stroke of 1906 while he was at Princeton. As a result, reading was difficult. He would often read with one eye covered. Prolonged reading often brought on headaches. See Weinstein, *Woodrow Wilson*, 164–68, 201, 250.

75 O'Shaughnessy, *Diplomat's Wife*, 258, 268–69, 275; and *Intimate Pages of Mexican History,* 306–32.

76 "Papers Relating to the Foreign Relations of the United States" (1914), vol. 1, 443–85. [hereafter *PRFRUS*]

77 Quirk, *An Affair of Honor,* 109.

78 House, *Diary,* April 15, 1914; also *PWW*, vol. 29, 448.

79 Bryan made clear to O'Shaughnessy that the president did not see U.S.

action as needing a congressional resolution, as it was not a war. April 21, 1914, in *PWW*, vol. 29, 478.

80   Lodge, "Congressional Record, 63rd Congress, 3rd Session, 1915,"p. 2650. Quoted in William C. Widenor, *Henry Cabot Lodge and the Search for an American Foreign Policy* (Berkeley: University of California Press, 1980).

81   Thomas Patterson, J. Garry Clifford, Kenneth J. Hagen, *American Foreign Policy: A History Since 1900* (Lexington, Mass.: Heath, 1991), 236.

82   Wilson, "Christ's Army" (See Appendix I).

83   Baker, *Life and Letters*, vol. 4, 289.

84   Quirk, *An Affair of Honor,* 154.

Chapter 3

1   Bryan to U.S. Ambassador to London, Walter Hines Page, July 28, 1914, in *PRFRUS,* 1914 Supplement, *The World War,* 19.

2   Ellen had arranged the meeting with Bryan that had brought him around to support Wilson.

3   Weinstein, *Woodrow Wilson,* 254–56.

4   To Mary Hulbert, August 2, 1914, in *PWW*, vol. 30, 327–28.

5   To J. R. Wilson Jr., August 6, 1914, in *PWW*, vol. 30, 351.

6   House, *Diary*, August 6, 1914.

7   To Mary Hulbert, August 7, 1914, in *PWW*, vol. 30, 357.

8   House, *Diary*, August 30, 1914; also *PWW*, vol. 30, 464–65.

9   House, *Diary*, November 14, 1914.

10   To House, August 17, 1914; also *PWW*, vol. 30, 390.

11   To House, August 18, 1914; also *PWW*, vol. 30, 395.

12   House, *Diary*, August 6, 1914.

13   House, *Diary*, January 25, 1915.

14   Wilson's need for female company is well documented. His own papers and journals note this. Literature on this, in addition to Weinstein, includes Phyllis Levin, *Edith and Woodrow.* The early psycho-histories (i.e., Freud/Bullitt and the Georges) have little or nothing to contribute to understanding of Wilson's relationship to House. A scathing refutation of the Freud/Bullitt book, *Can History Use Freud? The Case of Woodrow Wilson,* was written by Barbara Tuchman and printed in *The Atlantic,* February 1967.

15   House, *Diary*, November 14, 1914.

16   Millard J. Erickson, *Christian Theology* (Grand Rapids: Baker Books, 1985), 26 n. 22.

17   House, *Diary*, November 14, 1914.

18   See William Jennings Bryan, *Speeches of William Jennings Bryan, Revised and Arranged by Himself* (New York/London: Funk & Wagnalls, 1909). A discussion of the manner in which Bryan's religion effected his world mission

is found in Michael Kazin's book, *A Godly Hero: The Life of William Jennings Bryan* (New York: Knopf, 2006), 131–41.

19   Remarks to the Gridiron Club, December 11, 1915, in *PWW*, vol. 35, 344.

20   House, *Diary*, August 30, 1914; also *PWW*, vol. 30, 463.

21   House, *Diary*, December 17, 1914.

22   House, *Diary*, November 15, 1914.

23   House, *Diary*, November 25, 1914.

24   House, *Diary*, December 3, 1914.

25   House, *Diary*, November 7, 1914.

26   Wilson, *History of the American People*, vol. 4, 14.

27   Wilson's contemporary, British Prime Minister (1902–1905) Arthur Balfour noted the same principle but the opposite outcome. "Language is here no true or certain guide. . . . Men do not necessarily believe exactly the same thing because they express their convictions in exactly the same phrases." Wilson and Balfour represent the poles of optimism and pessimism regarding the ability of groups to agree upon the meaning of language. Balfour, *Theism and Humanism*, 150.

28   To House, August 3, 1914; also *PWW*, vol. 30, 336.

29   House, *Diary*, November 25, 1914.

30   Wilson, "Baccalaureate Sermon," June 9, 1907, *PWW*, vol. 17, 188–96.

31   "Baccalaureate Sermon," June 9, 1907, *PWW*, vol. 17, 195

32   "Appeal to the American People," August 18, 1914, in *PWW*, vol. 30, 394.

33   House, *Diary*, December 3, 1914.

34   Note from Gerard, September 10, 1915, in *PWW*, vol. 34, 441.

35   Mark Noll, *Princeton Theology*, 115, 157, 163–64.

36   House, *Diary*, August 30, 1914; also *PWW*, vol. 30, 462.

37   "On the Rural Church," December 10, 1915, in *PWW*, vol. 35, 330

38   To House, August 18, 1914; also *PWW*, vol. 30, 395.

39   House, *Diary*, August 30, 1914.

40   Lansing to Spring Rice, September 28, 1914, in *PWW*, vol. 31, 97–98; Bryan, Wilson and Lansing, September 30, 1914, in *PWW*, vol. 31, 103–4; Lansing to Page, October 16, 1914, in *PWW*, vol. 31, 161–63. John Coogan, *The End of Neutrality: The United States, Britain, and Maritime Rights, 1899–1915* (Ithaca: Cornell University Press, 1981), 187. See in addition, *PWW*, vol. 31, 110–11, 113–14, 125–26, 133–36.

41   House, *Diary*, September 30, 1914; also *PWW*, vol. 31, 108–9. The president compared the situation to the War of 1812, noting that the other U.S. president from Princeton, James Madison, had dealt with the situation differently.

42   "Remarks to the Associated Press in New York," April 19, 1915, in *PWW*, vol. 33, 38.

43 Isaiah 2:2-4 KJV.

44 "Remarks to Press," April 19, 1915, in *PWW*, vol. 33, 38–41.

45 House, *Diary*, September 29, 1914; also *PWW*, vol. 31, 108–9; "Remarks to Ohio Chamber of Commerce," December 10, 1915, in *PWW*, vol. 35, 321–22. See Coogan, *End of Neutrality*, 179–81.

46 December 10, 1915, in *PWW*, vol. 35, 327.

47 House, *Diary*, August 30, 1914; also *PWW*, vol. 30, 462.

48 House, *Diary*, November 25, 1914.

49 Memo to Tumulty, October 15, 1915, in *PWW*, vol. 35, 68.

50 Letter from House, November 10, 1915, in *PWW*, vol. 35, 186.

51 Wilson to Seth Low, November 8, 1915, in *PWW*, vol. 35, 180.

52 "Remarks to the Gridiron Club," December 11, 1915, in *PWW*, vol. 35, 343.

53 Ohio Chamber of Commerce, December 10, 1915, in *PWW*, vol. 35, 327.

54 "Remarks to the Gridiron Club," December 11, 1915, in *PWW*, vol. 35, 344.

55 Address to the DAR, October 11, 1915, in *PWW*, vol. 35, 49.

56 October 11, 1915, in *PWW*, vol. 35, 51

57 House, *Diary*, August 30, 1914.

58 House, *Diary*, November 25, 1914.

59 House, *Diary*, November 8, 1914.

60 "Remarks on the Navy Bill," August 29, 1916, in *PWW*, vol. 38, 101–2.

61 Examples of this are the series of addresses given between January 29 and 31, 1916, in *PWW*, vol. 36, 26–73.

62 Note speech on October 28, 1915, in *PWW*, vol. 35, 122–23; and the address to Congress on preparedness, in *PWW*, vol. 35, 297–302.

63 Weinstein, *Woodrow Wilson*, 282. Wilson Papers, May 9, 1915, in *PWW*, vol. 33, 127–38.

64 From House, May 9, 1915, in *PWW*, vol. 33, 134.

65 From Bryan, May 9, 1915, in *PWW*, vol. 33, 134–35.

66 Weinstein, *Woodrow Wilson*, 283.

67 Diary of Charles Lee Swem, May 10, 1915, in *PWW*, vol. 33, 138.

68 *PWW*, vol. 33, 449.

69 Address to newly naturalized citizens, Philadelphia, May 10, 1915, in *PWW* vol. 33, 147.

70 Address to newly naturalized citizens, Philadelphia, May 10, 1915, in *PWW*, vol. 33, 148–49.

71 Address to newly naturalized citizens, Philadelphia, May 10, 1915, in *PWW*, vol. 33, 149.

72 "Cruel and Inhuman Acts of War," May 25, 1915, in *The Papers of Robert Lansing*, Library of Congress microfilm.

73 "The Mentality of Woodrow Wilson," November 20, 1921, in *The Papers of Robert Lansing*, Library of Congress.

74 "The Mentality of Woodrow Wilson," November 20, 1921, in *The Papers of Robert Lansing*, Library of Congress.

75 "Address to the Federal Council of Churches," December 10, 1915, in *PWW*, vol. 35, 330.

76 See Phyllis Levin, *Edith and Woodrow*, 101–8. What House thought about Edith is largely lost to history. Before he died he tore a number of pages that he had written about Edith Wilson out of his diaries.

77 House, *Diary*, March 6, 1916; also *PWW*, vol. 36, 262.

78 House to Wilson, February 9, 1916, in *PWW*, vol. 36, 148.

79 Communications by J. J. Jusserand, J. Cambon, and A. Briand, February 9, 1916, in *PWW*, vol. 36, 149–50.

80 House to Wilson, February 9, 1916, in *PWW*, vol. 36, 148.

81 House, *Diary*, December 20, 1916; also *PWW*, vol. 40, 304–5.

82 House to Wilson, December 20, 1916, in *PWW*, vol. 40, 293–94.

83 Ohio Chamber of Commerce, December 10, 1915, in *PWW*, vol. 35, 327. Nordholt, *Woodrow Wilson,* 171.

84 Address to the League to Enforce Peace, May 27, 1916, in *PWW*, vol. 37, 113 –16.

85 *PWW*, vol. 35, 180–81. Nordholt, *Woodrow Wilson,* 183.

86 Note requesting a statement of war aims, December 17, 1916, in *PWW*, vol. 40, 273–76.

87 *PWW*, vol. 31, 459.

88 Address to Senate, January 22, 1917, in *PWW*, vol. 40, 536.

89 Lansing gave the Associated Press a paraphrase of the telegram on March 4, 1917, *Memorandum*, in *PWW*, vol. 41, 324.

90 War Message to Congress, April 2, 1917, in *PWW*, vol. 41, 527.

91 See Appendix 3.

92 August 17, 1876, in *PWW*, vol. 1, 180–81.

93 Woodrow Wilson, Fourteen Points Address to Congress, January 8, 1918, in *PWW*, vol. 45, 539.

Chapter 4

1 Note from German government, October 6, 1918, in *PWW*, vol. 51, 253.

2 Josephus Daniels, October 8, 1918, in *PWW,* vol. 51, 275.

3 Memorandum by Sir William Wiseman, October 16, 1918, in *PWW*, vol. 51, 347, 351.

4 To Robert Lansing, October 23, 1918, in *PWW*, vol. 51, 417–19.

5 Telegram to House from Wilson, November 17, 1918, *PWW*, in vol. 53, 108.

6 House, *Diary*, November 18, 1918; also *PWW*, in vol. 53, 109.

7   He would later refer to the treaty as coming not from human origin but "by the hand of God." Address to the Senate, July 10, 1919, in *PWW*, vol. 61, 436.

8   House and Lansing Memo, November 14, 18, 1918, in *PWW*, vol. 53, 71–73, 127–28.

9   House and Lansing Memo, November 14, 18, 1918, in *PWW*, vol. 53, 71–73, 127–28.

10 To House, October 13, 1917, in *PWW*, vol. 44, 378.

11 Sir William Wiseman, October 16, 1918, in *PWW*, vol. 51, 351.

12 House, *Diary*, December 17, 1918; also *PWW*, vol. 53, 417.

13 Wilson's Protestant theology would not have seen this language as referring to Peter, the "rock" of the Roman Catholic Church. Instead it would have been tied to two other places in scripture. The parable of the wise man who built his house upon a rock was the person who heard and acted on the words of Christ (Matt 7:24, Luke 6:48). Christ himself was the word, (John 1:1) thus to Wilson and his Presbyterian contemporaries it was Peter's confession that "Thou art the Christ the son of the living God" rather than Peter himself upon whom Christ would build the church. This could translate in Wilson's mind to the view that his Fourteen Points and League and Covenant of Nations, though a lesser word than Christ, were nevertheless divinely inspired and should be taken with a similar seriousness, a rock upon which a new way of international relations could be built.

14 Gustave Hervé, "Scruples of Mr. Wilson," March 25, 1917, in *PWW*, vol. 41, 466–67.

15 Note to Edward Park Davis, March 22, 1917, in *PWW*, vol. 41, 452–53.

16 Note to Edward Park Davis, March 22, 1917, in *PWW*, vol. 41, 452.

17 Cooper, *Warrior and the Priest*, 19.

18 For excellent background on the Hague treaties and the international system in place prior to the war, see Calvin Davis works on the Hague Peace Conferences.

19 To Theodore Marburg, March 8, 1918, in *PWW*, vol. 46, 572.

20 From House, March 8, 1918, in *PWW*, vol. 46, 574–75.

21 Robert Lansing, *The Big Four and Others of the Peace Conference* (Boston: Houghton Mifflin, 1921), 38, 40.

22 Lansing, *Big Four*, 46.

23 Wilson to Hoover, *Diary of Josephus Daniels*, October 17, 1918, in *PWW*, vol. 51, 372.

24 To House, July 21, 1917, in *PWW*, vol. 43, 238. *Diary of Josephus Daniels*, October 17, 1918, in *PWW*, vol. 51, 372.

25 Daniels, October 17, 1918, in *PWW*, vol. 51, 372.

26 Davis, *The United States and the Second Hague Peace Conference*, 326–59; MacMillan, *Paris 1919*, 42–43, 298–99, 492–93.

27	"Four Points Address," February 11, 1918, *PWW*, vol. 46, 320–21; Robert Lansing, *The Peace Negotiations: A Personal Narrative* (New York: Houghton Mifflin, 1921), 16, 77, 130.

28	Lansing Papers, *Desk Diary*, January 6, 1919; *Peace Negotiations*, 8, 190–204.

29	"Four Points Address," February 11, 1918, in *PWW*, vol. 46, 320–21.

30	Lansing, *Desk Diary*, January, 6, 1919.

31	Dr. Grayson, *Diary*, February, 22, 1919, in *PWW*, vol. 55, 224–25; Woodrow Wilson, "Remarks to the Democratic National Committee," February 28, 1919, in *PWW* vol. 55, 309–24.

32	See Appendix III.

33	Grayson, *Diary*, December 8, 1918, in *PWW*, vol. 53, 337.

34	Press Conference, *PWW*, vol. 50, 790.

35	Grayson, *Diary*, December 8, 1918, *PWW*, vol. 53, 337.

36	Grayson, *Diary*, December 8, 1918, *PWW*, vol. 53, 337.

37	Memorandum from the French Government, December 2, 1918, in *PWW*, vol. 53, 295.

38	House, *Diary*, December 16, 1918, January 7, 1919; also *PWW*, vol. 53, 401–2, 652–53.

39	Wilson to Cecil and House, cited in Davis, *The United States and the Second Hague Peace Conference*, 355.

40	Grayson, *Diary*, January 25, 1919; Note from House, January 25, 1919; Protocol of plenary session, January 25, 1919, in *PWW*, vol. 54, 262–63, 263–64, 264–71.

41	"Address at Metropolitan Opera House," March 4, 1919, in *PWW*, vol. 55, 418.

42	Paul Mantoux, *The Deliberations of the Council of Four (March 24–June 28, 1919)*, ed. and trans. by Arthur S. Link, vol. 1 (Princeton: Princeton University Press, 1992), 4–5.

43	Wilson, Statement on the Adriatic Question, April 23, 1919, in *PWW*, vol. 58, 7–8.

44	Orlando's Protest, April 24, 1919, in *PWW*, vol. 58, 97–101; Lansing, Memorandum, April 24, 1919, *PWW*, vol. 58, 102; House, *Diary*, April 24, 1919, *PWW*, vol. 58, 104; Tumulty, *Woodrow Wilson As I Know Him*, 105.

45	*PWW*, vol. 58, 5–8.

46	Lansing, *Peace Negotiations*, 82, 155; MacMillan, *Paris 1919*, 103; Clements, *Woodrow Wilson*, 200.

47	Further discussion, Michael D. Callahan, *Mandates and Empire: The League of Nations and Africa, 1914–1931* (Brighton/Portland, Ore.: Sussex Academic Press, 1999).

48	From Taft, March 18, 1919, in *PWW*, vol. 56, 83.

49 Lansing, *Big Four*, 51.
50 An good example of this somewhat simplistic reasoning on Wilson's part is the "Four Points Address to Congress," in *PWW*, vol. 46, 318–24.
51 John Foster Dulles, April 1, 1919, in *PWW*, vol. 56, 498–99.
52 John Foster Dulles, April 1, 1919, in *PWW*, vol. 56, 498–99.
53 Thomas William Lamont, April 1, 1919, in *PWW*, vol. 56, 502.
54 Quoted in Alan Sharp, *The Versailles Settlement: Peacemaking in Paris, 1919* (New York: St. Martin's Press, 1991), 14.
55 Quoted in Macmillan, *Paris 1919*, 18.
56 Keynes, *Economic Consequences*, 42–43.
57 February 11, 1918, in *PWW*, vol. 46, 321.
58 Keynes, *Economic Consequences*, 50.
59 Lansing, *Big Four*, 56–59.
60 Lansing, *Big Four*, 41.
61 Lansing, *Big Four*, 40–42.
62 Lansing, *Big Four*, 49.
63 House, *Diary*, June 29, 1919; also *PWW*, vol. 61, 354–55.
64 Wilson, Chamber of Commerce Speech, December 10, 1915, in *PWW*, vol. 35, 322–23.
65 Quoted in Hamilton Foley, *Woodrow Wilson's Case for the League of Nations* (Port Washington, N.Y.: Kennikat Press, 1967), 256.
66 Stid, *President as Statesman*, 152–53.
67 Wilson, "Congressional Government," January 24, 1885, in *PWW*, vol. 4, 13–179.
68 "Congressional Government," in *PWW*, vol. 4, 129.
69 "Congressional Government," in *PWW*, vol. 4, 129–30.
70 "Congressional Government," in *PWW*, vol. 4, 130.
71 "Congressional Government," in *PWW*, vol. 4, 130.
72 Wilson, "Constitutional Government," March 24, 1908, in *PWW*, vol. 18, 114.
73 "Congressional Government," in *PWW*, vol. 18, 106.
74 "Congressional Government," in *PWW*, vol. 18, 115.
75 "Congressional Government," in *PWW*, vol. 18, 115.
76 "Congressional Government," in *PWW*, vol. 18, 120.
77 To House, March 20, 1918, in *PWW*, vol. 47, 85.
78 Speech at the Metropolitan Opera House, March 4, 1919, in *PWW*, vol. 55, 415.
79 Press Conference, July 10, 1919, in *PWW*, col. 61, 423.
80 Press Conference, July 10, 1919, in *PWW*, vol. 61, 424.
81 Address to Senate, July 10, 1919, in *PWW*, vol. 61, 426–36.
82 Address to Senate, July 10, 1919, in *PWW*, vol. 61, 428.
83 Address to Senate, July 10, 1919, in *PWW*, vol. 61, 434.

84 Matthew 12:44, Luke 11:25.

85 Address to Senate, July 10, 1919, in *PWW*, vol. 61, 434.

86 Address to Senate, July 10, 1919, in *PWW*, vol. 61, 436.

87 Grayson, *Diary*, March 13, 1919, in *PWW*, vol. 55, 488 and footnote.

88 To House, March 19, 1919, in *PWW*, vol. 55, 499.

89 News Report, August 1, 1919, in *PWW*, vol. 62, 92.

90 Address to Congress, August 8, 1919, in *PWW*, vol. 62, 211–12.

91 News Report, August 2, 1919, in *PWW*, vol. 62, 112.

92 News Report, August 2, 1919, in *PWW*, vol. 62, 112.

93 *PWW*, vol. 62, 307. Reference to Matthew 5:18 and Luke 16:17.

94 Clements, *Woodrow Wilson*, 217; News Report, August 15, 1919, in *PWW*, vol. 61, 542.

95 Wiseman to Balfour, July 18, 1919, in *PWW*, vol. 61, 542.

96 Wiseman to Balfour, July 18, 1919, in *PWW*, vol. 61, 542.

97 Conference at the White House, August 19, 1919, in *PWW*, vol. 62, 355.

98 Wilson's instruction to Tumulty, May 9, 1919, in *PWW*, vol. 58, 1919; printed in *The New York Times*, May 10, 1919.

99 Conference at the White House, August 19, 1919, in *PWW*, vol. 62, 355–67.

100 Conference at the White House, August 19, 1919, in *PWW*, vol. 62, 361.

101 Conference at the White House, August 19, 1919, in *PWW*, vol. 62, 361.

102 2 Timothy 2:15.

103 Gene Smith, *When the Cheering Stopped: The Last Years of Woodrow Wilson* (New York: William Morrow, 1964), chap. 5.

104 Address in Kansas City, September 6, 1919, in *PWW*, vol. 63, 75.

105 Address in Helena, Montana, September 11, 1919, in *PWW*, vol. 63, 190.

106 Address in Columbus, September 4, 1919, in *PWW*, vol. 63.

107 Quoted in Phyllis Levin, *Edith and Woodrow*, 322, "National Republican," *WWPLC*, vol. 2, 105.

108 Address in Pueblo, Colorado, September 25, 1919, in *PWW*, vol. 63, 513.

109 Grayson, *Diary*, September 25, 1919, in *PWW*, vol. 63, 518.

110 Grayson, *Diary*, September 26, 1919, in *PWW*, vol. 63, 518–21. Cary T. Grayson, *Woodrow Wilson: An Intimate Memoir* (New York: Holt, Rinehart & Winston, 1960), 99–100; Tumulty, *Woodrow Wilson As I Know Him*, 446–48.

111 Link note, October 2, 1919, in *PWW*, vol. 63, 542 n. 1. See also *PWW*, vol. 63, Appendix I & II, 632–46.

112 More information on this period of the president's health can be found in Weinstein, *Woodrow Wilson*; Phyllis Levin, *Edith and Woodrow*; Smith, *When the Cheering Stopped*; Tumulty, *Woodrow Wilson as I Know Him*; Grayson, *Woodrow Wilson*; and *PWW* Vols. 63–68.

113 2 Corinthians 4:8-9 KJV.

114 Grayson's account, March 20, 1919, in *PWW*, vol. 65, 108–9; Smith, *When the Cheering Stopped,* 150; Grayson, *Woodrow Wilson*, 106, Clements, *Woodrow Wilson*, 220.

115 Grayson, *Woodrow Wilson,* 106.

116 James Kerney, last interview with Woodrow Wilson, in *PWW*, vol. 68, 589; Phyllis Levin, *Edith and Woodrow*, 488; Smith, *When the Cheering Stopped,* 226.

117 Quoted in Smith, *When the Cheering Stopped,* 219.

118 Margaret Wilson's discussion with her father, quoted in Smith, *When the Cheering Stopped,* 219.

119 Wilson to Samuel H. Thompson Jr., December 31, 1923, in *PWW*, vol. 68, 515.

120 Kerney, last interview with Woodrow Wilson, in *PWW*, vol. 68, 589.

121 News Report, November 11, 1923, in *PWW*, vol. 68, 469.

122 Herbert Hoover, *The Ordeal of Woodrow Wilson* (Washington, D.C.: Woodrow Wilson Center Press, 1992 [orig. publ.: New York: McGraw Hill, 1958]), 300.

123 Link, *Wilson*, vol. 2, 64–65.

Epilogue

1 "How the Democrats Got Religion," *Time Magazine*, July 23, 2007.

2 Richard M. Gamble, *The War for Righteousness* (Wilmington, Del.: ISI Books, 2003).

3 Reinhold Niebuhr, *The Irony of American History* (New York: Scribners, 1952), 63.

Bibliography

Manuscript and Microfilm Archives

The Papers of Ray Stannard Baker. Washington, D.C.: Library of Congress Photoduplication Service, 1982.

Papers Relating to the Foreign Relations of the United States. Washington, D.C.: United States Government Printing Office, 1931. [*PRFRUS*]

The Papers of Edward M. House. Manuscript and archives; microfilm reels 1–4. New Haven: Yale University Collection, 1913–1928.

The Papers of Robert Lansing. Diary, 9 vols. Washington, D.C.: Library of Congress Photoduplication Service, 1972.

Personal and Confidential Letters from Secretary of State Lansing to Woodrow Wilson. Washington, D.C.: Library of Congress Photoduplication Service, 1972.

The Presbyterian Historical Society Archives. Montreat, North Carolina.

Papers of Joseph Tumulty. Washington, D.C.: Library of Congress Photoduplication Service, 1975.

United States Department of State. *Records, Russia*, MF5206. Reels 1–7. Chicago: University of Chicago.

The Papers of Woodrow Wilson. Edited by Arthur S. Link. 60 vols. Princeton: Princeton University Press, 1966–1994. [*PWW*]

Woodrow Wilson Papers. Washington, D.C.: Library of Congress Photoduplication Service, 1972. [*WWPLC*]

The Public Papers of Woodrow Wilson. Edited by Ray Stannard Baker and William E. Dodd. New York: Harper & Brothers, 1927.

Unpublished Dissertations or Thesis

Benbow, Mark. "Leading Them to the Promised Land." Ph.D. Diss. Ohio University, 1999.

Callahan, Michael D. "International Law and the Neutrality of Belgium at the Outbreak of World War I." M.A. Thesis. Michigan State University, 1988.

Mooney, Michael. "Millennialism and Antichrist in New England, 1630–1760." Ph.D. Diss. Syracuse University, 1982.

Peters, Michael. "The Politicization of Jonathan Edwards' Millennialism." Ph.D. Diss. St. Louis University, 2000.

Published Primary Sources and Memoirs

Baker, Ray Stannard. *Woodrow Wilson Life and Letters: Youth 1856–1890.* Garden City, N.Y.: Doubleday, 1927.

Bryan, William Jennings. *Speeches of William Jennings Bryan, Revised and Arranged by Himself.* New York/London: Funk & Wagnalls, 1909.

Bryan, William Jennings, and Mary Baird Bryan. *The Memoirs of William Jennings Bryan.* Chicago: John C. Winston, 1925.

Bryan, William Jennings, and William Howard Taft. *World Peace.* New York: George H. Doran, 1917.

Daniels, Josephus. *The Life of Woodrow Wilson 1856–1924.* Philadelphia: The John C. Winston Company, 1924.

Grayson, Rear Admiral Cary T. *Woodrow Wilson: An Intimate Memoir.* New York: Holt, Rinehart & Winston, 1960.

Hoover, Herbert. *The Hoover Wilson Wartime Correspondence.* Edited by Francis William O'Brien. Ames: Iowa State University Press, 1974.

———. *The Ordeal of Woodrow Wilson.* Washington, D.C.: Woodrow Wilson Center Press, 1992. Originally published: New York: McGraw-Hill, 1958.

House, E. M. *The Intimate Papers of Colonel House*, vols. 1–4. Arranged by Charles Seymour. Boston: Houghton Mifflin, 1928.

Lansing, Robert. *The Big Four and Others of the Peace Conference.* Boston: Houghton Mifflin, 1921.

———. *The Peace Negotiations: A Personal Narrative.* New York: Houghton Mifflin, 1921.

———. *War Memoirs of Robert Lansing.* New York: Bobbs-Merrill, 1935.

Mantoux, Paul. *The Deliberations of the Council of Four (March 24–June 28, 1919).* Edited by Arthur S. Link. 2 vols. Princeton: Princeton University Press, 1992.

O'Shaughnessy, Edith. *A Diplomat's Wife in Mexico.* New York: Harper & Brothers, 1916.

———. *Intimate Pages of Mexican History.* New York: George H. Doran, 1920.

Thompson, Charles Willis. *Presidents I Have Known and Two Near Presidents.* Indianapolis: Bobbs-Merrill, 1929.

Tumulty, Joseph P. *Woodrow Wilson as I Know Him.* Garden City, N.Y.: Doubleday, 1921.

Warfield, Benjamin B. *Calvin's Doctrine of Creation: The Works of Benjamin Warfield,* vols. 1–10. New York: Oxford University Press, 1927–1932.

Westminster Confession of Faith. Atlanta: Committee for Christian Education & Publication, 1990.

Wilson, Woodrow. *Master Workers Book.* New York: Doubleday, 1916.

———. *Mere Literature.* Boston: Houghton Mifflin, 1896.

———. *A History of the American People,* vols. 1–10. New York: Harper & Brothers, 1901.

———. *A Crossroads of Freedom: The 1912 Campaign Speeches of Woodrow Wilson.* Edited by John Wells. New Haven: Yale University Press, 1956.

Works on Wilson, Wilson Era Politics, or International Relations

Ambrosius, Lloyd E. *Woodrow Wilson and the American Diplomatic Tradition.* Cambridge: Cambridge University Press, 1987.

———. *Wilsonianism: Woodrow Wilson and His Legacy in American Foreign Relations.* New York: Palgrave Macmillan, 2002.

Anderson, David D. *William Jennings Bryan.* Boston: Twayne, 1981.

Auchincloss, Louis. *Woodrow Wilson.* New York: Penguin Putnam, 2000.

Bailey, Thomas A. *Wilson and the Peacemakers.* New York: Macmillan, 1947.

Bailey, Thomas A., and Paul B. Ryan. *The Lusitania Disaster.* New York: The Free Press, 1975.

Bennett, John C., and Harvey Seifert. *U.S. Foreign Policy and Christian Ethics.* Philadelphia: Westminster Press, 1977.

Blum, John Morton. *The Republican Roosevelt.* Cambridge: Harvard University Press, 1965.

———. *Woodrow Wilson and the Politics of Morality.* Boston: Little, Brown, 1956.

Bragdon, Henry Wilkinson. *Woodrow Wilson: The Academic Years.* Cambridge, Mass.: Harvard University Press, 1967.

Buehrig, Edward H. *Woodrow Wilson and the Balance of Power.* Bloomington: Indiana University Press, 1955.

Callahan, Michael D. *Mandates and Empire: The League of Nations and Africa, 1914–1931.* Brighton/Portland, Ore.: Sussex Academic Press, 1999.

Clements, Kendrick A. *Woodrow Wilson: World Statesman.* Chicago: Ivan R. Dee, 1999.

Coogan, John W. *The End of Neutrality: The United States, Britain, and Maritime Rights, 1899–1915.* Ithaca: Cornell University Press, 1981.

Cooper, John Milton. *The Warrior and the Priest.* Cambridge, Mass.: Harvard University Press, 1983.

———. *Breaking the Heart of the World, Woodrow Wilson and the Fight for the League of Nations.* Cambridge, Mass.: Cambridge University Press, 2001.

Cooper, John Milton, and Charles E. Nev, eds. *The Wilson Era, Essays in Honor of Arthur S. Link.* Arlington Heights, Ill.: Harlan Davidson, 1991.

Craig, Hardin. *Woodrow Wilson at Princeton.* Norman: University of Oklahoma Press, 1960.

Davis, Calvin DeArmond. *The United States and the Second Hague Peace Conference, American Diplomacy and International Organization 1899–1914.* Durham, N.C.: Duke University Press, 1975.

Dos Passos, John. *Mr. Wilson's War.* New York: Doubleday, 1962.

Dosal, Paul J. *Doing Business with the Dictators: A Political History of United Fruit in Guatemala 1899–1944.* Wilmington, Del.: Scholarly Resources Books, 1993.

Foley, Hamilton. *Woodrow Wilson's Case for the League of Nations.* Port Washington, N.Y.: Kennikat Press, 1923.

Gamble, Richard M. *The War for Righteousness.* Wilmington, Del.: ISI Books, 2003.

George, Alexander L., and Juliette L.George. *Woodrow Wilson and Colonel House.* New York: Dover Publications, 1956.

Gregory, Ross. *The Origins of American Intervention in the First World War*. New York: W.W. Norton, 1971.

Hogan, Michael J. *Informal Entente: The Private Structure of Cooperation in Anglo-American Economic Diplomacy, 1918–1928*. Chicago: Imprint Publications, 1991.

Hunt, Michael H. *The Making of a Special Relationship: The United States and China to 1914*. New York: Columbia University Press, 1983.

Kazin, Michael. *A Godly Hero: The Life of William Jennings Bryan*. New York: Knopf, 2006.

Kelly, Alfred H., and Winfred A. Harbison. *The American Constitution, Its Origins and Development*. New York: W.W. Norton, 1970.

Kennan, George F. *Soviet-American Relations, 1917–1920*. Princeton: Princeton University Press, 1958.

Kettle, Michael. *The Allies and the Russian Collapse*. London: Andre Deutsch, 1981.

———. *The Road to Intervention*. London: Routledge, 1988.

Keylor, William R. *The Twentieth-Century World: An International History*. 4th ed. New York: Oxford University Press, 2001.

Keynes, John Maynard. *The Economic Consequences of the Peace*. New York: Harper & Row, 1920.

———. *Essays in Persuasion*. New York: Harcourt, Brace, 1932.

Kissinger, Henry. *Diplomacy*. New York: Simon & Schuster, 1994.

Knock, Thomas J. *To End All Wars: Woodrow Wilson and the Quest for a New World Order*. New York: Oxford University Press, 1992.

Levin, N. Gordon Jr. *Woodrow Wilson and World Politics*. New York: Oxford University Press, 1968.

Levin, Phyllis Lee. *Edith and Woodrow*. New York: Scribner, 2001.

Link, Arthur S. *American Epoch*. New York: Knopf, 1967.

———. *The Higher Realism of Woodrow Wilson*. Nashville: Vanderbilt University Press, 1971.

———. *Wilson*, 5 vols. Princeton: Princeton University Press, 1956.

———. *Woodrow Wilson: A Brief Biography*. Cleveland: World Publishing, 1963.

———. *Woodrow Wilson and the Progressive Era 1910–1917*. New York: Harper & Row, 1954.

MacMillan, Margaret. *Paris 1919: Six Months that Changed the World*. New York: Random House, 2001.

Martel, Gordon. *American Foreign Relations Reconsidered*. New York: Routledge, 1994.

May, Ernest R. *The World War and American Isolation, 1914–1917*. Cambridge: Harvard University Press, 1959.

May, Henry F. *The End of American Innocence*. London: Lowe & Brydone, 1959.

Mayer, Arno J. *Political Origins of the New Diplomacy, 1917–1918*. New York: Howard Fertig, 1969.

———. *Politics and Diplomacy of Peacemaking, Containment and Counterrevolution at Versailles, 1918–1919*. New York: Knopf, 1967.

McNamara, Robert S., and James G. Blight. *Wilson's Ghost*. New York: Public Affairs, 2001.

Mulder, John M. "Joseph Ruggles Wilson: Southern Presbyterian Patriarch." *Journal of Presbyterian History* 52 (1974): 245–71.

———. *Woodrow Wilson: The Years of Preparation*. Princeton: Princeton University Press, 1978.

Nordholt, Jan Willem Schulte. *Woodrow Wilson: A Life for World Peace*. Los Angeles: University of California Press, 1991.

Notter, Harley. *The Origins of the Foreign Policy of Woodrow Wilson*. Baltimore: The Johns Hopkins University Press, 1937.

Paterson, Thomas G., J. Garry Clifford, and Kenneth J. Hagan. *American Foreign Policy: A History Since 1900*. Washington, D.C.: Heath, 1991.

Preston, Andrew. "Bridging the Gap between the Sacred and the Secular in the History of American Foreign Relations." *The Journal of the Society for Historians of American Foreign Relations* 30, no. 5 (2006): 783–812.

Quirk, Robert. *An Affair of Honor*. Lexington: University of Kentucky Press, 1961.

Rich, Norman. *Great Power Diplomacy, 1814–1914*. New York: McGraw-Hill, 1992.

Seymour, Charles. *American Diplomacy During the World War*. Baltimore: The Johns Hopkins University Press, 1942.

Sharp, Alan. *The Versailles Settlement; Peacemaking in Paris, 1919*. New York: St. Martin's Press, 1991.

Smith, Gene. *When The Cheering Stopped: The Last Years of Woodrow Wilson*. New York: William Morrow, 1964.

Stid, Daniel D. *The President as Statesman: Woodrow Wilson and the Constitution*. Lawrence: University Press of Kansas, 1998.

Taylor, A. J. P. *The First World War*. New York: Perigee Books, 1980.

Thompson, John A. *Woodrow Wilson: Profiles in Power*. London/New York: Longman, 2002.

Thorsen, Niels Aage. *The Political Thought of Woodrow Wilson, 1875–1910*. Princeton: Princeton University Press, 1988.

Tuchman, Barbara. "Can History Use Freud? The Case of Woodrow Wilson." *The Atlantic Monthly*, February 1967.

———. *The Zimmermann Telegram*. London: Phoenix Press, 1958.

Walters, F. P. *A History of the League of Nations*. Oxford: Oxford University Press, 1952.

Walworth, Arthur. *Wilson and His Peacemakers: American Diplomacy at the Paris Peace Conference, 1919*. New York: W.W. Norton, 1986.

Weinstein, Edwin A. *Woodrow Wilson: A Medical and Psychological Biography*. Princeton: Princeton University Press, 1981.

Widenor, William C. *Henry Cabot Lodge and the Search for an American Foreign Policy*. Berkeley: University of California Press, 1980.

Works on Religious History or Political Philosophy

Ahlstrom, Sydney E. *A Religious History of the American People*. New Haven: Yale University Press, 1972.

Balfour, Arthur J. *The Foundations of Belief*. New York: Longmans, Green, 1895.

———. *Theism and Humanism*. Seattle: Inkling Books, 2000.

Berkhof, Louis. *Systematic Theology*. Grand Rapids: Wm. B. Eerdmans, 1991.

Boldt, John. *A Free Church a Holy Nation: Abraham Kuyper's American Public Theology*. Grand Rapids: Wm. B. Eerdmans, 2001.

Boyer, Paul. *When Time Shall Be No More*. Cambridge, Mass.: Harvard University Press, 1992.

Bouwsma, William J. *John Calvin, A Sixteenth-Century Portrait*. New York: Oxford University Press, 1988.

Calhoun, David B. *Princeton Seminary: Faith and Learning, 1812–1868*. Carlisle, Penn.: The Banner of Truth Trust, 1994.

———. *Princeton Seminary: The Majestic Testimony, 1869–1929*. Carlisle, Penn.: The Banner of Truth Trust, 1996.

Calvin, John. *Institutes of the Christian Religion*. Translated by Ford Lewis Battles. Philadelphia: Westminster Press, 1960.

Coalter, Milton J., John Mulder, and Louis Weeks. *The Organizational Revolution: Presbyterians and American Denominationalism.* Louisville, Ky.: Westminster/John Knox Press, 1992.

———. *The Presbyterian Predicament.* Louisville, Ky.: Westminster/John Knox Press, 1992.

———. *The Reforming Tradition, Presbyterians and Mainstream Protestantism.* Louisville, Ky.: Westminster/John Knox Press, 1992.

Crunden, Robert M. *Ministers of Reform: The Progressives Achievement in American Civilization.* New York: Basic Books, 1982.

Edwards, Jonathan. *The Works of Jonathan Edwards*, vols. 1–16. New Haven: Yale University Press, 1998.

Erickson, Millard J. *Christian Theology.* Grand Rapids: Baker, 1985.

Graham, W. Fred. *The Constructive Revolutionary: John Calvin and His Socio-Economic Impact.* Lansing: Michigan State University Press, 1987.

Hart, D. G., and Mark Noll. *Dictionary of the Presbyterian and Reformed Tradition in America.* Downers Grove, Ill.: InterVarsity, 1999.

Hatch, Nathan. *The Democratization of American Christianity.* New Haven: Yale University Press, 1989.

Hatch, Nathan, and Mark Noll. *The Bible In America.* New York: Oxford University Press, 1982.

Hegel, Georg W. F. *The Philosophy of History.* Translated by J. Sibree. New York: Dover Publications, 1956.

———. *The Philosophy of Right.* Translated by T. M. Knox. London: Oxford University Press, 1952.

Kemeny, P. C. *Princeton in the Nation's Service, Religious Ideals and Educational Practice, 1868–1928.* New York: Oxford University Press, 1998.

Marsden, George. *The Evangelical Mind and the New School Presbyterian Experience.* New Haven: Yale University Press, 1970.

May, Henry F. *Protestant Churches and Industrial America.* New York: Harper & Brothers, 1949.

McDermott, Gerald. *One Holy and Happy Society: The Public Theology of Jonathan Edwards.* University Park: Pennsylvania State University Press, 1992.

Morgan, Edmund S. *The Puritan Dilemma: The Story of John Winthrop.* Boston: Little, Brown, 1958.

Niebuhr, Reinhold. *The Irony of Athenian History.* New York: Scribners, 1952.

Noll, Mark A., ed. *Charles Hodge the Way of Life*. New York: Paulist Press, 1987.

————. *A History of Christianity in the United States and Canada*. Grand Rapids: Wm. B. Eerdmans, 1992.

————. *The Princeton Theology, 1812–1921*. Grand Rapids: Baker Book House, 1983.

————. *The Scandal of the Evangelical Mind*. Grand Rapids: Wm. B. Eerdmans, 1994.

Packer, J. I. *Evangelism and the Sovereignty of God*. Downers Grove, Ill.: InterVarsity, 1961.

Reichley, James A. *Religion in American Public Life*. Washington D.C.: The Brookings Institution, 1985.

Robertson, O. Palmer. *The Christ of the Covenants*. Phillipsburg, N.J.: Presbyterian & Reformed Publishing, 1980.

Ridderbos, Herman. *Paul: An Outline of His Theology*. Grand Rapids: Wm. B. Eerdmans, 1975.

Sandeen, Ernest R. *The Roots of Fundamentalism: British and American Millenarianism 1800–1930*. Chicago: University of Chicago Press, 1970.

Smith, Christian. *American Evangelicalism: Embattled and Thriving*. Chicago: University of Chicago Press, 1998.

Stoessinger, John G. *The Might of Nations*. New York: McGraw-Hill, 1990.

Strauss, Leo, and Joseph Cropsey, eds. *History of Political Philosophy*. Chicago: University of Chicago Press, 1987.

Walzer, Michael. *The Revolution of the Saints*. Cambridge, Mass.: Harvard University Press, 1965.

Tuveson, Ernest Lee. *Redeemer Nation: The Idea of America's Millennial Role*. Chicago: University of Chicago Press, 1968.

Wells, David F., ed. *The Princeton Theology*. Grand Rapids: Baker Book House, 1989.

————, ed. *Reformed Theology in America*. Grand Rapids: Baker Book House, 1997.

————. *Southern Reformed Theology*. Grand Rapids: Baker Book House, 1989.

Witherspoon, John. *The Selected Writings of John Witherspoon*. Edited by Thomas Miller. Edwardsville: Southern Illinois University Press, 1990.

————. *The Works of the Rev. John Witherspoon, D.D.L.L.D.*, vols. 1–4. Philadelphia: William W. Woodward, 1802.

Woodbridge, John D., Mark A. Noll, and Nathan O. Hatch. *The Gospel in America*. Grand Rapids: Zondervan, 1982.

Index

ABC Commission, 62; and negotiations, 62–63

Ambrosius, Lloyd E., 4–5

antinomy, 5, 18–24, 28–31, 47–48, 52–56, 63, 67, 69, 74, 77–81, 83, 86, 89, 100, 106, 109, 112–13, 157–58n39; and faith, 10–13

Armistice, 85–86, 93, 104, 113, 117

Balfour, Arthur, 158n39, 166n27

Bible, (scripture), W's views on, 11–12, 16, 18–22, 25, 36, 74, 76, 99, 111, 109

Bible, Address on the, 51–52

Blight, James G., 4

Bones, Helen, 67, 88

Britain, 73–75, 85–86, 93–95, 102

Bryan, William Jennings, 7, 41–42, 45–47, 53, 56–58, 60–61, 69, 75, 163n38, 164n79; and resignation, 77–80

Bryn Mawr, 14–16

Bush, George W., 115–16

Calvin, John, 11, 13–16, 157n19

Calvinist theological patterns, 18–21, 184–185, 66; and W., 2–5, 10, 13–27, 36, 50–52, 65–67, 74, 80, 105–106, 158n39; *see also* Presbyterian theological patterns

Carranza, Venustiano, 46, 49, 62–64

Cecil, Lord Robert, 92

China, 41, 44–46, 54

Christ's Army, 24–25, 44, 51, 63, 77, 84, 90, 106, Appendix I

Christian Statesman, A, 25–27

Christian statesman, 3–4, 13–16, 25–28, 36, 45–46

Civil War, effect on W, 4, 19, 34, 48, 51, 90

Clemenceau, Georges, 84, 94–95, 98

Clements, Kendrick A., 5, 163n38

concursus, 18, 67, 81, 157–158n39; *see also* antinomy

Congressional Government, 102–103

Constitution, W's views on, 69–70, 93, 99, 103–4, 109

185

need not be national always - need
not always understand. Be faithful +
do the right thing + God's intended outcome
will occur.
- predetermined view of the world, formed by
his religion.
WWI - opened up opportunities for his own
mission to bring God's order to the world.
- sermon to Princeton grads 1907
Redeemer attitude towards mediating peace
after/during WWI.
- america acts on behalf of the righteous.
Selfishness = sin p. 76
pgs 86+ Could no longer allow others
to do job correctly b/c it was his divine
mission.